Rock Garden Flower

or

Growing Up During the Depression

by

Florence Hardesty

Silver Tree Books　　　　　Silverton, Oregon

Silver Tree Books
Box 707
Silverton, OR 97381

© 2001 by Florence Hardesty
All rights reserved. Printed in USA

Publisher's Cataloging-in-Publication
(Provided by Quality Books, Inc.)

Hardesty, Florence
    Rock garden flower, or, Growing up during the Depression / by Florence Hardesty. -- 1st ed.
    p. cm.
    LCCN 00-110388
    ISBN: 0-9631769-3-5

    1. Hardesty, Florence. 2. Depressions--1929--Pennsylvania--New Castle--Personal narratives. 3. United States--History--1933-1945--Biography. 4. Nurses--United States--Biography. I. Title. II. Title: Growing up during the depression

F157.L3H37 2001   974.8'93'-092
                                   QBI00-902084

Cover by Bruce DeRoos
Layout and design by DIMI PRESS

Introduction and Acknowledgements

When I contemplated writing this book, I hoped to turn my vivid childhood memories into prose and carry you, the reader, to the scenes of my childhood and into the person of Little Flossie Fisher. But my seventy plus self, Florence Hardesty, kept interfering—commenting and adding information gained in the years since I was that child. Finally I decided to write it the way I would if we were sitting in my living room with a warm fire and a pot of tea. I hope you are happy with the result of that decision.

Any acknowledgement must include the three people who lived my childhood with me, my dear Mother, Floray Baird Fisher, and my beloved Father, Joseph Lemual Fisher. My brother, John Baird Fisher, traveled the longest with me along life's path. I dedicate this book to their memories.

My daughters, Susan Irvine and Shevawn Hardesty, who have declared me a lousy cook, have also decided that I really can write and have encouraged me. Thanks, girls.

My stepchildren, Kristi and Paul Holden have made what could be a difficult role easy. I am grateful.

The young people in my life have inspired me and as I have watched them grow, my childhood memories were stimulated. They are my Grandchildren, in order of appearance in the world, Leslie Irvine, Louis, George and John Arnos, and Daniel and Jeffrey Holden. My godchildren, Carmen and Louis Villegas have enriched my life. I especially hope that all you young people enjoy and learn from the book.

The people who helped me prepare and publish this book deserve thanks, Mary and Dick Lutz of Dimi Press and my editors, Cindy Wall, and her son, Robert Wall.

Finally, I must acknowledge the support and love so freely given by my husband, Verl Holden.

Chapter 1

At Grandma and Grandpa John's

My memories begin in 1930 when I was three. Mummy, Daddy, Johnny and I were living at Grandpa and Grandma John's house near New Castle, Pennsylvania. These grandparents, John and Florence Baird, had adopted my mother when she was four.

Grandpa John's younger brother, Tom and his wife, Alice were my mother's birth parents and had remained part of her and our lives. We called them Grandpa and Grandma Tom.

My parents were like millions of Americans in the early 1930s, living with relatives because they could no longer pay rent and feed themselves or their children. Even as a young child I was aware that my grandparents did not want us there.

Grandma John was a large woman with beautiful white wavy hair, cut in a mannish style. For some reason the long hair worn by most women her age at that time, was too much for her to cope with. She wore long-sleeved cotton dresses, aprons of a different print, cotton stockings and sensible shoes. She had a peculiar sour smell that increased as the time for her weekly bath approached. She spent most of the day sitting in a wicker rocking chair and talking to herself. You never had to wonder what Grandma John thought. All you had to do was listen. I didn't like her, and no wonder.

She called me Thelma more often than she called me Flossie. After calling me Thelma, she would say, "Flossie, I don't know why I call you Thelma. I never could abide that child."

Thelma was my mother's younger sister who had remained with her birth parents. She was charming and everyone loved her, which may explain why Aunt Florey didn't. What made all this even more strange was the fact that I had been named Florence Alice, after Grandma John and my birth grandmother, Alice Baird. Why, I wondered, couldn't that strange old woman remember my name when it was her own name.

Grandpa John had retired from farming a few years before. He and Grandma had rented their farm and moved to a brick bungalow that adjoined it. There was an acre of land with the house, fruit trees, grape arbors, a large garden, chicken coops and a barn. Grandpa kept a buggy and horse in the barn—no new fangled autos for John Baird.

There was a house across a garden from Grandpa's and a farm house across a field. The next nearest neighbors were a half mile down the road. From the front of Grandpa John's you looked out across a pasture, bordered by a split rail fence, to the knoll that held his original farm house and and the farm buildings. There was a field behind the bungalow, that was usually planted in wheat or corn. Down behind the barn where Grandpa kept his horse, there was a woods, that in summer yielded blackberries, strawberries and lovely fantasies. A little stream trickled through it.

Mother was a permissive mother who encouraged exploring, actual and intellectual. So even at three, I roamed the woods and fields adjoining the house.

An oil well pumped several hours a day on Grandpa's acre and many more wells dotted the farm across the road. The house was lit with natural gas from the wells which also powered the stove in the kitchen and the refrigerator on the enclosed porch. At that time the oil wells produced only fifteen or twenty dollars a month in income. However Grandpa had been a skilled framer and a shrewd spender. He and Aunt Florey were financially comfortable.

Grandpa was always pleasant to me. He wasn't openly affectionate but I knew that he liked me. He was a decent honest man who declared more than once in my presence, "My word is my bond." Every night, at bedtime, he read the Bible and ate warm bread and milk. He hadn't been to church in years, ever since the congregation had voted to remove the minister he liked. He remained the church's chief support, dutifully sending the largest donation it received, but never again attending.

Both Grandma and Grandpa John doted on my brother John. I was aware that I occupied second place in their affections but accepted it as normal. My parents loved me and that was enough.

Uncle John spent several hours a day in the chicken coop, reading the paper. When I discovered this, I thought he was avoiding our family. Years later I learned from my brother who spent many of his childhood summers there, that Grandma was the person he was avoiding when he spent time with his chickens.

It was obvious that Grandma and Grandpa John didn't like Daddy. Mother had met him at a Valentine's Day dance in 1923. She had been teaching in Youngstown, which was twenty miles away, across the Pennsylvania-Ohio border, and living in an apartment with other teachers, her college classmates. When she visited her parents, which wasn't often, she dated a young man from the neighborhood, and he and most of the people in the community thought that they had an understanding.

The April after they met, Mother brought Dad home to meet her parents. They were polite, but not warm. Grandpa walked them out to the car as they were leaving. He carried a lantern to light the way.

Mother suddenly said,"Uncle John, Joe and I are married." My Grandfather dropped the lantern. When I was grown she told me how sorry she was that she told him so abruptly.

My mother, Floray Baird Fisher, and Joseph

Florence Hardesty

Lemuel Fisher had been married by a minister in Youngstown on April 7, 1923. They had spent their honeymoon at a hotel in Cleveland. Mother had been twenty-six and Daddy thirty.

Years later, when their honeymoon hotel was being demolished, Mother bought a slab of marble that had been salvaged from the ruins and had a coffee table made from it. It must have been very important for her to preserve a souvenir of that occasion. The table now sits in my study.

My parents were attractive people. Both had dark hair and eyes. Mother had a slim figure with full breasts. She kept her figure all through her life. In college she had been voted the best dressed woman, and at that time she designed and made all her own clothes. Her dark hair was short in an era when bobbed hair was not quite proper. It lay in thick waves.

Daddy wore a slim mustache — he said he had it to draw attention away from a prominent nose — and he was movie star handsome. He was the son of Irish Catholic immigrants. His father, a hard coal miner, had developed silicosis and was unable to work. His mother moved the family from Pennsylvania to New Jersey where an older married daughter lived and sent the younger children to work in a glass factory to support the family. Dad's formal schooling ended at the end of third grade. His parents died within weeks of each other when he was fourteen. He lived for a time with older siblings. When he was a teenager he worked in the mines and was underground

At Grandma and Grandpa John's

when the roof of the shaft fell, filling much of the space. The donkey that was beside him was killed. He was physically safe, but the rest of his life he suffered nightmares in which he relived the experience.

Dad's parents had been poor and had little formal education, but there was culture in their home. They were well read and his mother and two brothers played the piano. Grandfather Fisher, also a John, loved opera and classical music.

When Dad left the mines he worked on the railroad and settled in Youngstown where his older brother lived. When mother met him, he was selling stocks and attending law school at night. One of the things that attracted her was his intelligence.

Dad had left the Catholic Church and married Mother in a Protestant ceremony. However to my Grandparents he was still suspect. This was the era when the Klu Klux Klan rallied against Catholics. Mother's parents would never have openly discriminated against another religion, but they weren't happy with Mother's choice.

Besides Dad's religious origin, he also was morally suspect. He liked to dance, he played cards and had an occasional glass of wine. Mother also did all this, but she had hidden it from her parents.

None of the older people in my mother's family understood the devastation brought by the 1929 market crash. They owned their farms, and their gardens and animals supplied food. Wood cut from their own trees kept them warm. They might have had difficulty selling their crops but they weren't hungry or in danger of being evicted. They needed money for oil for their lamps, salt to cure the meat and enough to pay doctor's and vet's bills. Some transactions could be handled through barter. They had enough savings to pay the taxes. The fact that my father was unable to support the family was to them proof that he was lazy or lacking in some way.

After my parents married they had lived in an apartment. Mother hid the fact that she was married from the school so she could continue teaching. Dad gave her a beautiful diamond ring and they bought sterling silver flatware and Haviland china. Daddy loved beautiful things as much as Mother. Reproductions of masterpieces hung on their walls and they had Persian carpets. Daddy appreciated fine glass, since he knew how difficult it was to make it.

Dad had dropped out of law school shortly after they were married. He had amassed the equivalent of a year's work by attending night school classes, when the school discovered that he didn't have the high school diploma that had been required for admission. The fact that he led the class didn't seem important; he was not allowed to continue. He kept his law books the rest of his life.

My parents moved from Youngstown to Warren, Pennsylvania. Johnny was born in February 1925 and I arrived in December 1926. Already they had begun to have financial problems. Mother wasn't working and Dad tended to live beyond their means. Mother had surgery for an ovarian cyst shortly after I was born. Johnny was an active two year old, whose favorite toy was a screw driver with which he unscrewed everything he found. Fortunately, I was, as my mother said "...a good baby who never cried and knew how to entertain herself."

I don't know why they moved to Schenectady in upstate New York. Dad was selling stocks or insurance and not doing very well.

Mother became pregnant again and Little Joseph Lemuel was born. When Mother first saw him, she laughed—he was a miniature of Dad. But after a few days in the hospital, it was apparent that something was wrong with this beautiful baby. He wouldn't eat and he seemed bruised. Mother wondered if the nurse had dropped him. When he was a week old, Little Joe died.

I have a vague memory of Dad carrying me to the hospital to see Mother. I don't know if it is a real memory or if I constructed it after I heard my mother tell a friend that she had been very depressed and the doctor had suggested that Dad bring me to visit her. Grandpa John had ridden the train to Schenectady and taken Johnny back to the farm with him.

Daddy did not have the money to pay Mother's hospital bill. The hospital wouldn't release her until it was paid. So he paid by check, took Mother home and then stopped payment.

I never learned what had happened to Little Joe's body.

Mother and Dad weren't alone in having financial problems. All across the country, families faced similar situations. My husband, Verl Holden, was born in his grandparents' farmhouse. There were twenty two adults and a number of children living there, family who had come home because they had no work and no place to live. One person, his grandfather, had a job.

A favorite story of Mother's was about how the neighbors in the apartment building where she and Dad lived had foiled the loan company who came to take a family's furniture. The helpful neighbors obtained a key to the apartment and moved out all the furniture, dispersing it among themselves. Then each of them contributed their oldest object and furnished the apartment with castoffs. This was done without the apartment owners or loan company's knowledge. So the loan company got a truckload of castoffs and then the neighbors refurnished the apartment with the original pieces.

Such moments of triumph were few. By the time my memories began, we were at my Grandpa Johns, with nothing but our clothes.

Mother and Dad spent much of the day together. Most of my memories involve being outside in the summer time, playing with Johnny. Grandma John sat in the living room in her rocking chair, rocking and carrying on her solitary conversation. Grandpa would be in the garden or chicken coop.

Johnny and I loved each other a great deal later in our lives, and there are family stories about how protective Johnny was with his little sister, Bossie Bisser, but my memories of those summer days do not contain the love and compassion that bonded us later. I was the pesky little sister and he was the mean older brother.

We were active kids. A window was broken that led to a crawl space under the house. I think Johnny broke it. I remember crawling through it and exploring the dark, damp space, which was draped with spider webs and paved with the skeletons of little animals who had been trapped. It was a great adventure for a three year old. On the way out, I cut my leg on the glass and bled profusely which frightened my parents.

Another vivid memory concerns the only time I defeated my brother in physical combat. I don't know what started it but John was winning. He had me prone on the grass and was sitting on me; he pinned my hands to the ground with his, and with his other two hands, he pounded my face. Wait a minute, says my adult rational mind; no human has four hands. So my memory is inaccurate, but that is what it felt like.

I looked up at him and wondered, should I or shouldn't I?

I did. I lifted up my head and bit his nose as hard as I could. He screamed, blood spurted and he leaped up and ran to Daddy for comfort. I don't remember being punished.

Although Grandpa's house was in the country there was another house across a garden and Junior Reese lived there. He was a year older than I and he and Johnny were soon fast friends. I played with them some but most of the time I was not welcome.

I remember the peeing contests we had. We stood

on Junior's high porch and saw who could pee the farthest. Not being properly equipped, I lost every contest.

Another time I tagged after the boys as they ran to the outhouse. They went inside and closed the door. When I demanded to be admitted, Junior told me to put my fingers in the crack by the hinges, made because the door was not quite shut. Silly me. I did. Then he closed the door crushing my fingers.

Years later when we were high school classmates and Junior was the class heart throb, I still hated him.

I abandoned the effort to become one of the gang and fell back on my own resources. We had no radio and television had not been invented. I remember two books, a very old hardcover *Mother Goose* and *A Child's Garden of Verses*. I had memorized them so I assume that I had been read to.

I do remember Dad reading aloud from *One Hundred and One Famous Poems*. He had a beautiful rich voice and I would sit on his knee while he read. When he wasn't there, I would pick up the book and read to myself. I knew the poems by then and would recognize the correct pages by the authors' photos. I began to associate the words in my mind with the words on the page. Later I scanned the newspaper looking for words I knew and guessed at others. I'm not sure that my parents were aware of my new found skill.

I wandered around grandpa's acre with a special friend, a little blue plush bunny. We talked and told each other stories. When I made myself an apple blossom crown and played bride, blue bunny was my groom. We climbed the apple tree together and looked down on the world below. He was a far more agreeable companion than Johnny or Junior.

And then I lost him. I looked everywhere. I searched through the woods calling his name. At night I imagined him alone in the dark, frightened and crying for me. My heart ached for him.

A long time later when I had ceased mourning for my friend, I found him. He was in the barn on a shelf. When I picked him up the blue plush failed and wet sawdust poured out. I looked at that heap of sawdust and ragged plush and was empty of feeling. He wasn't my friend or even a toy—just damp sawdust and a rag.

I was barefoot all summer. I had been warned to avoid the bees that buzzed around the flowers and the clover in the lawn. I was out by the rose bushes when I noticed a very small bee sitting on a clover blossom. I thought about the warnings. Then I lifted up my foot and stamped on the bee. Mother was right! Hot agony pierced my foot and I went screaming for comfort. That was a painful but valuable lesson—*Listen To Your Mother.*

My parents spent most of the day together. At night Mother and I slept in the guest room. Dad slept on a day bed in the dining room, alone because he had fewer nightmares when he was undisturbed, I don't know where Johnny slept, perhaps with Grandpa in his room.

We all ate together on the big round table on the back porch. Mother did most of the cooking because Aunt Florey wasn't well. Her malady was never diagnosed but she belched loudly, particularly at the table.

I sat in the high chair. I remember one dinner vividly. I kept getting up and standing in the chair. My parents told me repeatedly to sit down. Finally my exasperated father got up, snatched me out of the high chair, took me outside and paddled me. It was the first time I had ever been disciplined physically. I wailed and screamed, not because I was hurt, but because I was outraged that my Daddy would spank me. I did stop standing in the high chair, however.

Even as a child, I wondered how a nice man like Grandpa John happened to be married to Aunt Florey. Years later I learned about my grandparent's courtship. It seemed that Grandpa had called on Aunt Florey for a time, and then stopped visiting. She became ill and the general consensus was that it was a broken heart. Her father, a wealthy German farmer, Andrew Hoffmaster, called on Grandpa and they talked.

John resumed his courtship and married her. They moved to a farm which his father-in-law deeded to them. A generation earlier it had been part of the original Baird farm which had been divided and sold. As time passed Florey became increasingly strange. But Grandpa John, a man of his word, was always a faithful loving husband. When Mother was four, they adopted her. Then her birth parents moved onto an adjoining farm that Grandpa John had owned and which he deeded to them.

All of her life my mother struggled with the question, "How could her mother have let her be raised by such a strange woman?" Yet her mother was always involved with her. Mother contracted typhoid fever when she was a teenager, and her birth mother nursed her for months. When Mother went to high school she lived in New Castle with her birth grandmother, a wise and wonderful woman who had emigrated from England. Three of her aunts lived on the same street and she spent a great deal of time with them.

There had been a time when Mother's birth parents had been separated. Grandpa Tom spent some time in the West. It is possible that the adoption occurred then. Mother had three younger siblings, William and Thelma who were just a few years younger, and James who was fifteen years younger.

Was mother traded for a farm? Did Grandpa John receive a farm for marrying Aunt Florey? It is very likely that the answer to both questions is, "Yes."

I'm not sure how long we were at Grandma and Grandpa John's. We were there in the Spring and Summer. The first Christmas I remember was there. I had turned four a few weeks before. Everyone I might have asked for exact dates has died.

As a young child I knew we were not welcome, only tolerated. Now that I am an adult I can appreciate how difficult it must have been for my grandparents to have a young family, the man of which they disliked, move into their home. Then I felt only rejection from them. But I also learned what for me was a valuable response. I learned to disregard the people who had negative feelings toward me. My mother loved me and my father adored me. If they weren't there, I had myself. As long as I had myself there could be other blue bunnies when I needed them.

Chapter 2

At Grandma and Grandpa Tom's

Sometime that winter or Spring, we left Grandma and Grandpa John's. Dad went to Youngstown and Mother, Johnny and I went to the farm of my mother's birth parents. I don't know what caused us to leave but I know Daddy wasn't with us because he wasn't welcome.

Grandma and Grandpa Tom Baird lived on a farm a few miles from the tiny village of Princeton. The farm house was big and comfortable. Out back there was a large barn and the usual farm outbuildings. Cows, pigs, horses and chickens inhabited the fields and pens. A large garden and orchard were near the house and the surrounding fields and woods stretched to the horizon.

My memories of being there are set in summer or autumn. In the summer, the place swarmed with people. My cousins, Billy and Jackie Lusk, Aunt Thelma's children were there. Young Bill and Donnie Baird, my Uncle Bill's boys completed the cousin group. The boys, with the exception of Donny who was a few months younger than I, were two to four years older than Johnny.

At Grandma and Grandpa Tom's

Andrew Baird, the older brother of the Baird men lived with my grandparents. He was twenty years older than Grandpa Tom. I remember him as a bent old man with white hair and a beard. He seemed ancient to me, but four-year-olds are poor judges of age.

Grandma Tom dressed much like Aunt Florey although she was a much smaller woman. She smelled of laundry soap and bleach. Her salt and pepper hair was pulled back into a bun. I don't think I ever saw her smile. At four I was a little wary of her, but I didn't dislike her as I did Aunt Florey. Years later, when I was a young married woman, Grandma and I enjoyed each other. She had mellowed and I had matured.

Grandpa Tom was warm and witty. He had dark eyes that sparkled especially when he was teasing someone. His teasing was always gentle, never cruel, and was one of the ways he expressed love. His hair was gray and he had a thick bushy mustache.

Grandma had been quoted as saying that when she married him, he was the best looking man in Lawrence County. Even at four I believed that. Someone else said that Grandma had been a lovely blue-eyed blonde. When I heard that, I marveled.

Grandpa did the farm work, assisted by the grandsons. I don't think they really helped much. The oldest of the group was ten and the youngest four. However, they trailed around after Grandpa and he gave them tasks to perform. Most of the time they played in the barn or on a makeshift ball field.

Mother's younger brother James was a teenager. He was an attractive young man with curly blonde hair and blue eyes. He delighted in teaching little ditties and poems to Johnny and me. The poems were mildly dirty, not pornographic but in bad taste. Jimmy hoped that we would recite them in company and shock the adults. When he was doing this, Grandma would speak sharply, "James, stop doing that!" There would be a pause in the lessons, but only a pause. We learned them and used them to amuse the other children but Johnny and I were too wise to repeat them when adults were present.

I also had chores to do. Every day, I dusted the large farm house. The living room was filled with the sort of objects you see in catalogs with Victorian themes. This was to be expected since Grandma had been born in England. I patiently dusted bronze knights, colored glass and English bone china. The stuffed coon, a tribute to a taxidermist's art, intrigued me, although he smelled a little musty.

My other chore was picking green beans. Every day I picked a mess of beans and snapped them. Grandma cooked them until they were soft, flavoring them with bacon grease. As I remember, they were the main dish for both dinner and supper. Would you believe it, my favorite vegetable to this day is green beans.

I had no better luck fitting into the boys group than I did with Johnny and Junior. I wandered around the farm and amused myself. I have one distinct memory of a bright cool day. It must have been Fall. Clouds moved swiftly across the intense blue sky and when the sun was obscured it was chilly. Around the side of the house, close to some hydrangea bushes the chickens had made some indentations in the ground where they dusted themselves. When the sun disappeared behind the cloud, I lowered myself into a depression snuggled close to the earth and kept warm. I'm sure I needed a bath that night.

I also remember sitting on the high bank that overlooked the road that ran by the farm. The ground was covered with a creeping weed that had little blue flowers. I watched the dusty road below, looking for cars, hoping that one would be Daddy's.

I didn't know then that my grandparents had forbade Daddy from visiting. Years later Mother told me that Daddy was living in a rooming house in Youngstown and trying to make a living by selling Real Silk underwear door to door. He had no automobile. At one point his landlady wrote to Mother and said that he was so depressed, she was afraid he would kill himself. Mother called him and they arranged to meet. Daddy walked thirty miles to the farm and met her in the woods.

I did join the boys, one time, in their favorite amusement, teasing Uncle Andy. The game went like this. You called the old man names, and then ran as fast as possible to a ladder that led to the roof of the chicken coop. Andy's part in this drama was to swear at them and wave his cane. Foolishly I joined the boys. Only I didn't run as fast as they did and I was the last one to reach the ladder. I never got to the roof. Uncle Andy plucked me off the ladder and paddled me. I cried so long and hard that the adults were frightened.

I suppose that my grief over my father's absence and the awareness of my Mother's sorrow combined and burst forth in a torrent of tears. Uncle Andy walked three miles to Princeton to buy candy and gifts to atone. And the adults put an end to the boys' game.

Aunt Thelma's husband, Jack Lusk, was doing very well despite the depression. He was a supervisor of the region's A&Ps, Atlantic and Pacific Food Stores. The company was a large chain that before the advent of the supermarket had grocery stores in every town. He drove a big Buick and he and Aunt Thelma belonged to the country club. Uncle Jack had plans to go into business for himself as soon as he could find backers. Grandma and Grandpa were very impressed with his success. I'm sure that in their eyes, compared to Jack, my warm nurturing father was a complete failure.

Aunt Thelma was charming. She was full of stories about cocktail parties and the important people she met. She and Uncle Jack owned a colonial home, which was beautifully decorated. At times she had struggled with serious health problems, but at this period, she was always gay and sunny. It must have been difficult for my mother, dealing with our situation while her little sister was so self satisfied.

Someone told the man Mother had dated before she married Daddy, that my parents were separated. He came to visit. Mother told him that they were separated only geographically and that she was committed to her marriage. Years later he was admitted to the hospital where I worked as a nurse. He had a brain abcess at the site of a brain tumor that had been removed shortly after Mother married Dad. His parents had blamed Mother for his illness.

I remarked that I thought he had known my mother, Floray Baird Fisher. He glared at me and turned his face to the wall. I was a very young nurse. I soon learned to approach delicate subjects more cautiously. I was also glad this man had not become my stepfather.

There was a one room school a mile down the dirt road from the farm. Mother was hired to teach there. Married women weren't usually hired as teachers. Perhaps because Daddy wasn't living with us an exception was made. Mother had graduated from normal school, Slippery Rock State, and then gone to summer school at Penn State until she obtained a degree. She was also an experienced teacher. Even with so many people out of work, this school would have had trouble attracting such a well prepared teacher.

When Fall came, Mother left every morning with Johnny, a first grader, in tow to walk the mile to the school. I was left with Grandma.

Johnny had a hard time at school. The other boys put him up to engaging in pranks—such as putting a snake in mother's desk drawer. Mother wasn't bothered by the snake, only by her son's behavior. So she paddled Johnny. Corporal punishment was acceptable in those days. When Grandma heard about it from a neighbor, she paddled Johnny too.

John had difficulty learning to read. Mother was as much a reading specialist as was available at that time. She tried to teach him in the evenings after dinner. But John would burst into tears when he didn't know the words. My heart ached for him. I was careful to hide my own ability to read, which seemed to have come with no effort.

Grandma decided to break me of a bad habit. I sucked my thumb. My favorite was my left, but in a pinch my right would do. Mother was relaxed about my comforting habit. She had studied the psychology of John Dewey and talked a lot about readiness. She was sure that I would give up my thumb when I was ready. But she didn't have the energy to argue with Grandma, so I was subjected to the treatment.

The first assault on my habit was something that tasted so bitter, that after three score and ten years, my mouth still puckers with the thought. But Little Flossie was not to be deterred! I just sucked until the foul tasting stuff was gone.

Next came the splint treatment. Both my arms were splinted so that my hands couldn't reach my mouth. I slept with Mother and I was, and am, a great cuddler. Mother must have thought she was sleeping with Pinocchio. But not to worry, I wiggled and picked and soon the splints were gone.

The third effort was the mitt treatment. Both hands were bundled tightly into mitts. Once again, I managed to free my hands and plop my left thumb into my mouth.

Finally sharp springs were attached to the mitts. That was the last. Grandma gave up. My thumb continued to be my faithful friend, along with a worn quilt I called my pretty cover for several more years.

When I began school, at rest periods when the teacher told us to put our heads on our arms at the desk, I sucked. After a day or so my addiction was discovered. It took only a little teasing and I went cold turkey and gave up my thumb. Peer pressure is much more powerful than grandma pressure.

That Fall, something wonderful happened. Daddy got a job. Uncle Jack used his influence and Daddy was hired to be the manager of an A&P store in Kopple, a small steel town in the Beaver River Valley, north of Pittsburgh.

Chapter 3

Together Again

It was night but the kitchen was illuminated by golden light. An oil lamp hung above the table, and the cook stove in the corner warmed us. The room glowed with the happiness and love. The family was together again.

Mother and Dad had rented a small house about two miles down the road from my Grandparents' farm, and a mile from the school where Mother taught. The furniture and precious things that they had been able to keep had been stored and now they were happily unpacking the boxes. Daddy carried them in from his new car. I'm sorry I don't know the kind of auto and Johnny, who would know, has been dead for several years. Mother was unpacking her china.

She held a cup up to the light. I later learned it was Rani by Haviland. "Oh Joe, it is so beautiful. I'm so glad we got this pattern."

"Yes Dear, I must admit I like it better than the

flashy pattern I wanted when we bought it. You do have good taste. I just wish we still had the sterling to go with it."

"The silver plate is fine, and I won't have to count it every time we entertain, like I did the sterling."

Daddy came over and gave Mother a little kiss. They hadn't done that when we were at either of my grandparents' homes. Then he disappeared out the door for another load.

He brought in a doll stroller. I didn't remember it although there was a picture in the photo album of a toddler pushing it. Was that me? I wondered.

"Here Flossie, here is your baby doll stroller. Maybe I'll find your doll soon."

The next box contained crystal. Dad began to unpack it. He held the goblets up to the lamp and admired them. Later when I learned that he had spent his childhood working in a glass factory, I understood his fascination with fine glassware.

I left the kitchen and went into the living room to explore. I had been there that afternoon when Daddy showed me the room. Now it was illuminated by an oil lamp that sat on a marble and brass table.

A graceful sofa stood in front of the windows and there was a wing chair in a corner. A chair Daddy had called a Windsor chair stood in another. A deep blue rug with a golden border covered the floor in front of the couch. A picture of a young boy, dressed in a blue suit looked down at me from the wall above the fireplace. Daddy had said his name was Blue Boy by someone whose name I had forgotten. Now I know it was Gainsborough. There were other pictures that Dad had pointed out to me and told me their names and who had painted them.

A bookcase filled with books stood along one wall. I had never seen so many, even at Mother's school. Dad had a set of the Harvard Classics and many of the law books he had used when he was in school. Mother also had the books she had used in college, and all of the titles I later studied in Literature class. My favorite book was on the table, the well worn *One Hundred and One Famous Poems*.

It was obvious that this room and the objects in it were very special to my parents. How difficult it must have been to live in someone else's home and be separated from all of their treasures.

The bedroom off the kitchen was furnished with a full bed, a dresser and a vanity. They were dark shiny wood and all matched. It was cold in there. The only heat in the house came from the stove in the kitchen or a fire in the fireplace.

Even colder was a room just off the bedroom. It had a low sloped roof, as though it had been added to the house as an afterthought. It held a metal bed and a dresser. There were hooks along the wall to hold clothes.

That night the sleeping arrangement became clear. I had been afraid that Johnny and I would be forced to sleep in that cold little room. Instead I slept with Mother and Johnny and Daddy bedded down under piles of blankets in the shed-like room. I heard Mother explain it to the neighbor girl the next day. "It is so cold in the bedrooms that Joe and I each sleep with a child to keep them covered and warm."

There was no bathroom. Each bedroom had an enameled pot with a cover that was used during the night and emptied every morning. The outhouse was about two hundred feet away, down a stone path through the garden. There were two holes in the bench so one could be companionable while taking care of business. Mother insisted on toilet paper so the Sears Catalog was only for entertainment—or an emergency. In the summer the little building smelled and the flies were pesky and in the winter the wind blew up the holes and frosted one's anatomy. I had no interest in company or tarrying when I made a trek to the outhouse.

A pump on the open back porch supplied water. In the winter it was frozen and it was necessary to pour boiling water on it before the long iron handle could be moved to produce a flood of icy water. The porch also served as the wood shed.

The kitchen was large and bright. In addition to the coal stove, there was a dry sink, table and chairs and a day bed. Washing of hands, bodies, and dishes took place in various basins in the dry sink.

Milk and meat were set outside on the porch in a wooden box with a lid. We didn't have an icebox and if we had, I doubt that any ice men would come so far out into the country to deliver ice.

By today's standards, the little house in Princeton was barely adequate for human habitation. But after living as an unwelcome guest in my grandparents' homes, it seemed like a palace to me.

The next morning, Daddy left long before daylight to drive to his job in Koppel. Mother dragged a reluctant Johnny out from his cocoon of blankets and the two of them dressed warmly and donning heavy coats and galoshes set off down the road to the school. Mother had hired an eighth grade boy who lived near the school to arrive early and start the fire so the room would be warm when she and the children arrived.

A neighbor girl was hired to babysit me. She lived in a house behind our garden and had finished the eighth grade a few years before. I don't remember her name and have no memories of us doing anything together. As Mother said, "Flossie knows how to entertain herself" and once again I proved her right.

What I remember most about what we called the little house in Princeton was how happy we all were. Both parents had a glow about them and they spoke to each other using terms of endearment. Dad addressed Mother as Dear. (The man who owned the little grocery store in Princeton thought her name was Dear Fisher.) When Mother said Joe it had a special ring to it.

When I was an adult and Mother and I spoke as two women, she told me that she and Daddy had a very passionate and satisfying sexual relationship all during their marriage. In fact that was one of the things that held them together when the relationship was strained by the stress of the depression. Our strange sleeping arrangement didn't seem to deter them from being together sexually. Maybe that was the reason for the day bed in the kitchen.

The A&P where Daddy worked was open late on Saturday night so he arrived home long after we were in bed. If Uncle Jack happened to be visiting, he was even later. Dad enjoyed a drink occasionally but I never saw him drunk. However, alcohol was becoming a major problem for Uncle Jack. I heard Daddy tell Mother that one reason he stayed out with Jack was to see that he got home safely.

Since Dad wasn't there to warm up the bed for Johnny, he slept with Mother and me. Dad would join us on Sunday morning and the family would enjoy a cuddle fest. We would talk, tell stories and laugh. One of the adults would have added wood to the kitchen stove and kindled the fire in the fireplace to warm the house.

One Sunday morning when Dad opened the door of his cold little room and crossed the icy linoleum to join us, we heard a scratching sound and then a wiggling furry ball was dumped onto the bed.

It was a chow puppy. Chows were the fashionable breed in 1931 and Uncle Jack had bought several—too many for Aunt Thelma. Chum Lee, Chummy, was our new dog, and my faithful companion.

I have memories of roaming about the fields adjacent to the house, making adventures in my imagination. I also had a spot near the kitchen stove where I played with paper images of people that I had cut from Mother's magazines. I made a house from a cardboard box, created furniture from empty tin cans and match boxes and made up my own fairy tales. As an adult I have looked at Barbie and Ken and thought, "They sure would have lasted longer than my paper people."

Florence Hardesty

Since my parents had to pump the water on the porch, haul it into the house, heat it on the stove and wash the clothes by hand, changes of clothing were as infrequent as possible. Wintertime baths and hair washing were events. Dad wore starched white shirts, which he washed and ironed himself and Mother was always well groomed. But I was attracted to dirt and apparently the attraction was mutual.

What did little girls wear in 1931? I remember distinctly because I was frustrated when I dressed myself. In winter I wore one piece long underwear. There was a flap that buttoned across the back at the waist line. It took time to undo it and was hard to rebutton. I'll let the reader imagine what happened when I delayed the cold trip to the outhouse and then made a mad dash down the snow-covered path.

Over my underwear I wore a panty-waist. That extinct garment was a muslin vest, with buttons in the front. It had four long tabs extending to the top of the thighs, at the end of which was a fastener the purpose of which was to hold up stockings. My fasteners were frequently lost and large safety pins took their place.

Brown cotton stockings were the next item of apparel. The trick was to smooth out the long underwear, hold it tight to one's ankles and pull the stockings up over it. If I let go, the underwear bunched up and bagged around my knees. In any case, wrinkle free extremities were rare. A slip was pulled on next.

Mother was an expert seamstress. She had studied home economics at Penn State during the summers of the first years she taught school. Sewing, design and tailoring had been included in the course. There were attractions other than classes at Penn State. She told me there were seven men to each coed and besides it gave her an excuse to be away from Aunt Florey and the farm. Later her skill and education served the family well. At Princeton she made my dresses and they were well made, usually with an empire waist covered in smocking.

My dresses were pretty but I hated my underwear and stockings. I remember one glorious Spring day. It must have been the first warm day. I was in a field near the house, playing alone, as usual. I hung my coat and hat on a bush at the edge of the field, took off my shoes and stockings, rolled up my underwear, and danced in the tall grass. That moment is one of my happiest childhood memories.

What did I wear in summer? Not much. The underwear was exchanged for underpants. Johnny's cast off overalls were my play uniform. Some were bib overalls but most were onepiece coveralls with sleeves. Since Johnny was hard on his clothing, the elbows and knees usually had worn through and the sleeves and legs had been chopped off. We were barefoot all summer.

Johnny and I were plopped into a wash tub by the kitchen stove, or stood on the dry sink and sponged down each night. We did go to bed clean.

My father's older brother, Jim Fisher, came to visit and brought his oldest son, Clyde. Jim was a musician, a ragtime pianist. He had had a dance band and played in silent movie theaters. Mother and Dad had met at a dance where he was playing. Uncle Jim and Aunt Grace had three children, Clyde, James Michael or Mickey and a baby, Marilyn. They had owned a home and at one point a theater. By now they, like so many others, had lost it all. The younger children were with their mother at her relatives in Pittsburgh.

Clyde was about twelve, a handsome boy whose dark good looks were like my Father's. He was well read and had quick intelligence. He had had rheumatic fever and it left him with a damaged heart. He had been instructed not to swim or engage in sports, an instruction he defied. After a few days, Uncle Jim left and Clyde stayed with us.

Clyde obeyed the house rules but there was an aura of anger about him. Now, I think how difficult it must have been to have been driven to unknown relatives and dumped. He and Johnny played together and I watched from a distance.

Clyde was fascinated by snakes. He spent time in the nearby swamps catching them. He put them in orange crates with glass over the top. They seemed to like their new homes but frequently escaped from the boxes and sunned themselves on the glass. Clyde and Johnny would let them out, stand on the porch, and dangle objects down at the snakes to induce them to strike. That was one time I didn't want to join the boys' games.

After several months, Uncle Jim returned and Clyde left with him. A few years later he spent some time with us, but that is the last time I saw him. He struck out on his own when he was about fifteen. He occasionally had a sudden loss of consciousness and would be picked up off the street and taken to a hospital. When he was old enough, the hospital hired him and he became an orderly. Eventually he moved to California and met a nurse in the hospital where he worked. They married and had several children. He died when he was in his forties.

Johnny and I played more happily together than we had in the past. Maybe that was because there was no one else to play with. Our parents had been reading to us about cavemen. It fascinated us to think that people had once lived outside, with only a cave for shelter and a bonfire for warmth. So we decided to play caveman, inside. We crawled behind the couch and made it our cave. Then John took some embers from the fireplace to emulate a fire. Fortunately Mother discovered this before any damage was done. That was the second time my parents paddled me, and my first experience with Dad's razor strap.

One Saturday, Johnny induced me to join him on an expedition to the swamps to see if we could capture some of the creatures who lived there. Dad had released Clyde's snakes when the zoo keeper left. I wasn't interested in snakes but I did like frogs and salamanders. We didn't tell Mother where we were going and we got lost. I don't remember if we were successful in our collecting. Finally, we found our way back to the house, cold, wet and after dinner. My was Mother mad!

She made us change our wet clothing and sat us down to eat. That being accomplished it was time for punishment. The instrument was Dad's razor strap, the leather device on which Dad sharpened his straight razor. There were two straps to it. When it was swung one hit the other with a loud splat. Now, thank goodness, men use safety or electric razors and homes no longer contain these instruments of terror.

Mother grabbed John's arm and swung the strap against his protesting rear. Memory is not always accurate. As I remember Mother stood in the middle of the kitchen and Johnny ran around her. Each time he got into the proper position, she swung the strap. I know she must have been holding his arm and as he tried to escape they turned. I sat on the couch and felt guilty. Poor Johnny was being paddled and I was just as guilty as he. Mother relieved my guilt. She grabbed my arm, said, "You too!" and applied the strap.

That was the third of four times in my life that my mother hit me. Johnny was not so lucky. I watched him being punished for transgressions and foolishness and learned early to avoid such pain. I just made sure I didn't bother my parents with my sins. I dealt with the consequences myself.

My first real Christmas was at the little house in Princeton. There had been a Christmas at Uncle John's and Aunt Florey's, but it had been a surprise. I woke up one morning and there was a decorated tree on the sun porch and a doll that had been left for me. After that experience, I knew what Christmas was. I knew the story of the Christ Child, but more important, I'm sorry to say, was that Santa would come and bring gifts. I was in a frenzy of anticipation as I waited for the day.

I went to bed alone on Christmas Eve and lay in the dark, ears straining for a sound. There would be no sleep for me when that Jolly Old Elf came down my chimney. After a while I heard the sound of his reindeer on the roof, then silence. I know now it must have been heavy snow sliding off the pitched roof. I called to my Mother, "He's gone. Can I come and see?"

What could she say but yes? The tree was beautiful. There were no lights because we had no electricity but the ornaments shone in the light of the oil lamp and the fire. My presents were books and crayons, wonderful treasures.

Come to think of it, Christmas is still my favorite time, and the anticipation only heightens the pleasure. My birthday is December Sixth, St. Nicholas Day. So the bleakest time of the year is the month I celebrate most.

The school year was ending and my parents had made the decision to move to Koppel where Dad was working. I was five and Johnny seven. For all the rest of our lives, the year we spent in the little house in Princeton was cherished in our memories. It was the year we were together again.

Chapter 4

Life In Town, The Yellow House

In 1932, Koppel was a town of about 1000 people. It is forty miles north of Pittsburgh in the valley of the Beaver River, a tributary of the Ohio. It is twenty miles south of New Castle, a small city not far from Grandpa John's.

The Koppel Car Works, a German owned company, was the only industry in the town and was the reason for the town's existence. The plant and the rail yard lay close to the river and the town was spread up a gentle slope from it for five or six blocks. The cross streets were a little longer. A single railroad track ran through the center of the town.

Some of the houses were comfortable brick and wood homes along tree-shaded streets. Several other blocks had smaller identical houses, company houses, and finally there were several blocks of row houses. The row houses were weathered gray when I saw them, and were called pumpkin row by the town's people. When they were first built they had been painted orange with green trim.

There was an air of disappointment about the town. Streets defined blocks that were empty of buildings and filled with weeds and scrubby trees. The two block long business section held empty buildings and the few stores that existed. Mud and debris covered the vacant lots between the buildings.

The yellow brick school had four rooms that housed the upper grades. It was surrounded by barracks-like buildings where students in the first four grades were schooled.

The town seemed like a metropolis to Johnny and me. I could remember living only in the country. John may have remembered Schenectady but that was a long time before.

We called our new home the yellow house because that was the color of the paint. It sat on the second lot of an otherwise empty block. In the back yard there was a garage opening onto the alley, and grape vines and fruit trees. The first lot on the block was occupied by Mr. Bartett's chicken coop, the residents of which crowed and clucked their greetings. The school buildings were behind us, across the alley. A large building that resembled a house was diagonally across the intersection. It was the American Legion Hall. In the basement, reached by a separate entrance was the German Club, a supposedly private club that served beer to anyone known to the patrons. The rest of that block was a gravel street shaded with maple trees and lined with pleasant houses.

Young woods and brush —willow, maple, sumac and blackberries—had grown up on empty lots on our block. Across the street the woods had been cleared and gardens planted.

The furniture had been moved and placed before John and I arrived. Daddy stopped the car in front of the house so we could get a better view. Then the car doors burst open and two eager kids and a furry dog spilled out and ran up the steps to the porch. We tried out the swing while Daddy unlocked the door. Mother was away when we arrived.

We dashed into the entry hall. Johnny vaulted up the stairs with Chummy at his heels. I went through an archway into the living room. It was light and comfortably furnished with the treasures from Princeton's little house. Blueboy smiled down from above the fireplace. There was one new addition in the room, a Philco radio. It was a table model and soon would become a source of great pleasure. I don't know if it was new or if it was another of my parent's possessions that had been stored.

The dining room was behind the living room. A drop leaf table made of beautiful cherry wood stood in the center. It also was something I hadn't seen before. The kitchen was large and bright. In front of the window sat a sturdy table and chairs, painted bright apple green. There was a gas stove and, wonder of wonders, a real sink with hot and cold running water. The linoleum and walls were also green. It looked fresh and new that day but two years later the entire family had developed a lifelong antipathy to that shade of green. The back door led to a little shed that held an ice box and Chummy's bed.

Upstairs, there were three bedrooms. Two were furnished and the third was filled with boxes and crates. It was supposed to become a bedroom for Johnny or me. However, we lived in the house for four years and furniture was never bought for it. We continued our strange sleeping arrangement.

The bathroom, with its sink, toilet and large bathtub was viewed with delight. There would be no more icy trips to the outhouse or sweltering episodes of elimination accompanied by the buzz of flies.

The stairs off the kitchen led to a full basement with a large fruit cellar.

We had loved the little house in Princeton because it was ours and we were together. But the yellow house seemed like a mansion.

It was summer and evening was falling but it was still light. Johnny and I decided to explore the town. My brother had been there before and said that he would show me Daddy's store. I don't remember if we told our parents that we were going.

In any case, we started out down the street, past the little candy and tobacco store on the next corner and the police station half a block to the right. We crossed the railroad tracks and headed down another street. The light faded and soon it was dark. We passed the row houses and then turned back. Johnny was sure he knew where we were going. We both were a little worried but not panicked. After all, we had found our way out of a swamp in Princeton.

We rounded a corner and there was a large man with a badge on his chest. He asked who we were

Florence Hardesty

and we told him. We said we were looking for Daddy's store. He said that he knew Daddy and then he walked us home.

So our first night in Koppel we were lost—but rescued.

Years later when Mother and I lived in Cleveland a family moved in behind us. Suddenly it seemed there was a swarm of children everywhere, in our garage, on the neighbors porch and in the flower bed. Mother said, "Those are country kids. They aren't used to living in town."

She was right. When we met the parents we learned they had just moved from a farm in upstate New York. I smiled as I remembered when Johnny and I had been country kids, newly located in town.

We settled into the town quickly. Johnny was seven and he roamed farther than I. However, I was free to explore. In the early 1930s, parents weren't expected to keep close track of where their children were or what they were doing.

My first friends were the Bartett girls. I met them when their father came to feed table scraps to the chickens. Regina and Gilberta were my age and a year older, friendly little girls who spoke only French. That didn't seem to be a handicap because we played happily together. They lived a short block away, down the road beside the Legion Hall, across the railroad tracks on a street of company houses.

I spent a great deal of time at their house. Mrs. Bartett told my mother that I was learning a little French. One time it seemed I understood her when she uttered the French equivalent to "I wish that kid would go home." I apologized for staying too long and left.

Several years later our friendship came to an end. Regina told me that she had been born from a rose and Gilberta came out of a cabbage. Johnny heard this and proceeded to set them straight. He said that he had seen a calf being born and knew that our suddenly fat cat had kittens in her belly. Mrs. Bartett came out on the porch and shrieked at him in French. It took several years for the lady to forgive us and by that time I had other friends.

Mrs. DeSanzo lived in the first house on the next block. An aura of tragedy surrounded her and she dressed in a dull black dress, the mourning garb of the Italian women of the town. She wasn't mourning the death of anyone, but the absence of her husband. He had lost his job at the plant and became so delusional that he was committed to a mental hospital in Pittsburgh. He had been there several years and had not improved. She had two teenaged sons and a three year old, Sonny.

Mrs. DeSanzo was very welcoming and seemed to enjoy my company. I spent many hours in her house. She had a shrine to the Blessed Virgin in her darkened bedroom, lit by candles in red glass containers. She went up to pray often and invited me along. Her prayers had an edge of desperation. They were in English and I soon knew them well.

Even now, more than sixty years later, when I'm frightened I pray the Rosary and the Lord's Prayer with the same desperate cadence Mrs. DeSanzo used. I am happy to report that the plane has always landed safely, the car wreck was avoided and I've gotten off the roller coaster alive. Thanks, Mrs. D.

Sonny was the most rotten spoiled three year old I had, and have, ever met. He was always indulged and never corrected. My other friend, Betty Jean Little, lived beside the DeSanzo's. One time, with his mother's permission, we took Sonny for a walk in the woods. Once out of his mother's and our parents sight, we threatened the little monster with dire consequences if he didn't stop hitting us, taking our toys and being genuinely awful. He cried and cried. We had a hard time calming him down so we could return, but we were firm in our threats. My, was Sonny glad to see his mother! And he was such a nice little boy when Betty Jean and I were present. Mrs. DeSanzo said we were such good influences.

Johnny was hard on my toys. He took my doll carriage and turned it into a vehicle for himself. He rode it down the terrace in front of the house, usually ending in the ditch. I screamed in protest but no one came to the rescue of the toy, and in a day it was ruined.

Since I couldn't beat John up physically, I found other ways to get even. I wrote his name on the side of the house with crayon. I made the letters the way he made his. Dad delivered a reprimand, his usual, "God Damn it, John.....", and I smirked at my brother.

The year of security and happiness was over. Not long after we moved to Koppel, Daddy lost his job.

The man who had expected to become manager was his assistant, and may have been taking notes about Dad's performance. Perhaps someone higher in the hierarchy than Uncle Jack needed a job for a relative. But knowing Dad, the fault probably lay in his inability to take orders from people he considered his intellectual inferiors.

I had heard him tell Mother that he ordered more fish on Friday than he could reasonably expect to be sold. Then as Saturday wore on toward closing time, he sold them for very little because they would be spoiled by Monday. For some of the town's families that was the only protein they ate. It may have been charitable, but he had been hired to make money for the company.

Mother assumed a worried look that became a permanent part of her. Dad focused his energy on the "God Damn A&P", or his assistant who may have tattled on him. Mom worried about how we were going to live.

There was no work available. There was no relief and the WPA had not yet begun. We had rent to pay, coal and electricity to buy and we needed to eat. Mother got an occasional day of work as a substitute teacher, but that wasn't enough. Neither set of grandparents would give us any money. They would have taken Mother, Johnny and me back into their home, but that man who wouldn't work, my adored father, could not have gone with us.

We weren't alone. The car works had been shut down and all the men had been laid off. The beauty

Florence Hardesty

shop, barbershop, theater, and all the garages but one had closed for lack of business. The men played bocci ball and tended their gardens. The women worried. Half the town's adults had been born in Europe and the parents of most of the rest had also been immigrants. There was still a great deal of anti-immigrant, anti-catholic feeling in the country. Occasionally one would hear the suggestion that we should "....send all those Dagos, Hunkies and Polocks back to where they came from." People were anxious to become citizens. Most of the men had learned English, forced by the necessity of their jobs. The woman who had been at home, caring for the children had little opportunity to learn. The priest spoke their language and they socialized with people from their original county.

Mother had studied French and German in high school and college. She was more comfortable in German but she could manage with French. In the years after World War I, she had taught ungraded classes of immigrant children. She taught them English and when they were ready moved them into the regular classrooms. In the process she picked up a few words of Italian and Greek.

Mother spread word around town that she would be teaching English and Citizenship classes in our home. Soon, several afternoons a week, the living and dining room would be filled with the women of the town. Those who had a little money paid her. Others brought food from their gardens. The woman who had a cow supplied milk and cottage cheese. The

Italian women kept us in tomato sauce and tomatoes. For years after, I wore a soft wool head scarf, maroon with a border of roses, that one of Mother's students had brought from Italy when she came. One large Russian woman offered to clean our house.

They progressed rapidly. When they passed the test and were citizens, they had a request. They wanted to learn the manners and social customs of America. Mother was happy to oblige.

Roosevelt had become President and he was moving rapidly to help the desperate people of the country. There was hope that there soon would be relief and jobs. But in the meanwhile, Mother used her education and ingenuity to feed us.

Chapter 5

My Parents Manage to Feed Us and I Learn About the World

I began school that September in one of the temporary buildings not far from my back door. Miss Broadbeck was my teacher and like many first-graders, I loved her for her patient kindness. There must have been thirty children in the room and she was very busy. I sat quietly at my desk and had very little to say.

A pair of twin girls with dark curly hair sat beside me. They were dressed in fluffy ruffled dresses as though they were going to a party. They must never have seen school supplies before. They diligently gnawed away their crayons. Then they wet their pants. The teacher conferred with the principal and it was learned that they were only four. They didn't come back.

A boy on the other side of me had black hair and intense dark eyes. He was dressed in wool knickers, stockings and a long sleeved shirt. Poor Anthony, he smelled of urine. The teacher moved him to a spot near the open window.

We children were alert and eager to learn. The teacher passed out our primer. I opened it up and read about Dick, Jane and their dog, Spot. I thought it was pretty dull and not nearly so interesting as *"The Owl and the Pussy Cat"*. The teacher never realized that I could already read. When I was called upon to read, I did and then sat down in my seat and day dreamed. I was a good little girl and she had her hands full with the other students.

Mother, who had been Johnny's teacher had passed him conditionally. He was in second grade, making friends and doing seven year old things. I was accustomed to spending time alone. At lunch time, I often went down the road to the woods and explored. I picked trilliums and pussy willows in the Spring and berries in the Fall. The woods were my own special place.

After a few weeks I got acquainted with the rest of the class. Bernadine Brunner looked like a travel folder for the Tyrol, all neat braids and starched dirndls. I was rather fond of Joe Nardone. Yolanda Izzo had blonde curls, big dark eyes and lots of ruffles. About a quarter of the room had last names that ended in ski, and fully half ended in an a or o. Catherine Roberts and Glen Marshall were the only students who were not products of families who had left Europe in this or the last generation.

Most of my learning came at home. Every evening Daddy and Mother read to us. Mother had a list of the children's classics. She would read a chapter and then Daddy would read another. We savored *Hans Brinker and the Silver Skates, Heidi, Tom Sawyer, Treasure Island, Huckleberry Finn, Little Women, Little Men, Robinson Crusoe, Swiss Family Robinson* etc. We may have been poor, but we were rich in those moments. When my parents' voices were tired and the book was closed and placed on the table, I would pick it up and silently try to go on. Johnny, eager to know what happened next, would beg me to read aloud. Before long I read a third chapter every evening.

My parents loved and knew poetry. Anything might stimulate the recitation of a poem. A dark rainy day and Mother, who'd be washing dishes or ironing, would recite, "The day is cold and dark and dreary, The wind is wild and never weary...." The sight of flowers would bring forth any number of poems.

We went to visit the Grandparents every Sunday. I'm not sure if it was because we enjoyed their company or the fact that they often sent us home with eggs, milk, meat from the smoke house and fruit. In the car, Mother and Daddy would have declaiming contests. Dad would recite the Declaration of Independence and the Constitution. Yes, the whole thing! Mother would show off with Lincoln's Second Inaugural Address. In between we would have Shakespeare.

Since gasoline was precious, a substance to be preserved, we coasted down every hill. We would make bets about how far we could go. Johnny and I would yell, "The third fence post," or "The big tree." and then we'd will the car to make it, even grunting with effort.

Sometimes our car fun was a little crude. Someone would fart. Then someone else would accuse the culprit, or the culprit would make the accusation. We'd all enjoy the game.

Not all our rides were so pleasant. When Daddy was in a bad mood, he spent the trip swearing at the other drivers for their ineptness. He would go on about politics or someone he was annoyed with in blistering fashion. This was termed yammering and when that happened, Johnny and I sat in the back seat and withdrew into ourselves.

One time we were making a trip to Pittsburgh. This usually was a rare treat. However this time Daddy yammered all the way through the Beaver Valley. Now there is a freeway. Then it meant going forty miles through one small steel town after another. We got to downtown Pittsburgh and stopped for a red light, a stimulus for more cursing. Mother, without saying a word, got out of the car and disappeared in the crowd. Dad had to move on. He went around the block, parked and looked for her. She had disappeared. Then one subdued man and two scared kids rode home to Koppel. Shortly after we got there, Mother walked in. She refused explanation. That stopped the yammering—for a while.

The radio was a source of pleasure. John and I listened to Tom Mix, Little Orphan Annie, and Jack Armstrong, the All American Boy. The episodes were

Florence Hardesty

short, fifteen minutes but they seemed to pack a lot of adventure into a short time. We also listened to the Joe Louis-Max Baer fight. Father Coughlin was a radical priest whose fascist views my father loved to hate. In order to discount his position, we had to hear what he said. We heard Hitler's speeches and the ecstatic screams of his followers.

The radio also provided music. We listened to the opera on Saturday mornings and the NBC Symphony on Saturday night. The news was also an important part of our lives. KDKA Pittsburgh was the station that provided so much pleasure.

No one else on the street had a radio and so when there was an important broadcast we had company.

Abruptly the reading and listening ceased. Our electricity was turned off. The landlord didn't evict us for non-payment of rent because there were no other tenants available and an empty house might be vandalized. Mother's students and the grandparents kept us in food. Dad picked up coal from along the railroad tracks and so the house was warm. But the power company had strict policies—no pay, no power.

Then Uncle Jim Fisher came to visit. He had electrical skills. He went to work and added a circuit to our electrical line that by-passed the meter. It could be turned off and on with a switch. He instructed Dad to scrape together enough money to pay the bill and have the power turned back on. Then we were to use the bypass switch when ironing, running the sweeper or some other power consuming activity took place.

We weren't to use it at night when someone might notice that the lights were on and the meter wasn't working.

I don't know how my parents obtained the money. They must have sold something. And once again we enjoyed our nightly reading and the radio.

I had my first and last escapade of thievery when we lived in the yellow house. I asked Mother for some money to go to the candy store at the end of the block. She said that she had no money. I knew that this was not true. I had looked in her purse and there were two silver coins, one very small and a larger one. She had lied to me, I told myself, righteously and went to the bedroom opened the purse and took a coin. I took the smaller one, the dime, and left her the big one, the nickel.

I went into the store and woke the proprietor who slept at one of the tables in the back. Usually the kids stole a piece of gum or a candy bar before they woke him, but I didn't need to. I had money. I got a large bag of candy for such a small bit of silver.

Suddenly I was the most popular little girl on the block. Surrounded by a crowd of taffy chewing youngsters, I headed home. The candy seemed to lose its savor with every step and the tight grip of shame moved across my chest. Then an older child came running down the street toward me. "Flossie, your mother is looking for you."

My sweet toothed followers abandoned me and I went home to meet my fate. Mother had been saving that fifteen cents to make a payment for something from the church. When a woman came to deliver the object, Mother discovered my theft. She told me how embarrassed and humiliated she had been. I was in agony with guilt.

Wise Mother, she didn't relieve that guilt by spanking me. I don't think I have ever stolen anything since.

I'm not sure how long no one in the household had employment and now there is no one to ask. Perhaps the sense of desperation that I sensed from my parents enlarged the time period in my memory.

Two men came to repossess Daddy's car. It was all paid for save for the last $15 payment. Fortunately Dad was at home. He told the men that they would have to kill him before he'd let them take the car. They left.

That night we were reading in the living room. Suzie, Chummy's sister, had been added to the household and was sleeping on the floor. Chummy was outside in his pen which was attached to the side of the garage. The fence that contained him was as high as the eaves. Chummy was an escape artist but finally Dad had him in what he thought was a secure pen.

Suddenly, Suzie jumped up and began to bark. She ran to the dining room window, knocked over a large fern in front of it and tore down the curtains with her paws. Dad grabbed her collar and restrained her from going through the window.

Then he ran outside. Chummy was out of his pen. Somehow he had climbed the fence. There was some torn cloth with blood on it on the ground and the lock to the garage door had been broken.

The car was never repossessed. Chummy was our hero.

But Chummy was not the neighbor's hero. He never bothered people but he did fight with and even kill other dogs—and cats. Mother was very embarrassed about this but there was little she could do with Dad. She was the daughter of a farmer who had raised sheep. Those farmers routinely killed stray dogs who might chase and kill the sheep. Dad's attitude must have been hard for her.

Every day Chummy made his rounds. One call was made to the police station where he lifted his leg and marked the entrance. He developed a limp and we suspected that he might have been shot in the hip.

Chows are intensely protective and loyal. They have a hierarchy in their affection and loyalty. Dad came first, then me, Johnny and finally Mother. Mother had to shut up the dogs if she wanted to punish us. John and I soon learned that when the dogs were present, not to scream or run when we played with our friends.

One time after Mother did get a job, she was on the bus on her way to work when the bus stopped. A large chow, Chummy, was sleeping in a sunny spot on the pavement. The driver and the other people on the bus were afraid to get out and chase him off the road. Mother was too embarrassed to let them know it was her dog. Finally he got up, stretched and ambled off.

Chummy finally met his match. He was chasing a chicken down the railroad tracks and ignored a train. He ended up in two pieces. Johnny was terribly upset and tried to move the parts so that the body appeared whole. Fortunately, I didn't see the accident.

Suzie was hit by a car and that was the end of the canine section of the family. We acquired cats and the neighbors were surely relieved.

The first Christmas in Koppel I received a teddy bear. Mother had sent me upstairs to get her shoes and there on the closet shelf was teddy. I claimed him early and that was the end of my belief in Santa Claus.

The second Christmas in Koppel was our most desperate time. As the day approached, Johnny and I grew more excited. One night after our reading session, our parents told us that this year Christmas would have to be skipped. There was no money at all and there would be no tree, no presents, no candy and no special meal. Johnny and I already knew that Santa was a myth created by parents, but we hoped that somehow he did exist. My parents' sad faces drove away that hope.

The day before Christmas, Dad walked to the post office to pick up the mail. There was a letter from Alice Casey, one of mother's college roommates. Dad put it on the table for Mother.

It was dark when Mother got home from the house of one of her students. She crunched through the snow to our house, trying not to notice the Christmas lights in the windows on the street. She saw Alice's letter before she took off her coat and opened it with anticipation. Alice was a loved friend.

"Joe, Johnny, Flossie, get ready. We have to get to Beaver Falls before the stores close. Alice sent money. We are going to have Christmas!"

The letter contained a ten dollar bill. We got a Christmas tree, the fixings for a feast and presents for Johnny and me. We children waited in the car while our parents went into the toy store. It seemed as though they were in there forever. When they came out they had a red fire truck for Johnny and a stuffed Scottie dog for me. I named the dog Bobby Burns, after the poet, and for the next three years he was one of my closest friends.

An announcement was published that investigators would be hired to help administer a new federal relief agency. Both Mother and Dad applied and took the Civil Service Exam. Both passed the test with high scores, but only Mother was hired. Dad was angry that he had been passed over but we all were glad that someone was working.

Mother took the bus to Beaver Falls every weekday. She had never learned to drive. I remember sitting in the back seat, a tight little ball of fear, while Dad tried to teach her. Her lessons always ended in tears. Almost thirty years later, after Dad died, she learned to drive and drove all over the United States.

Driving was a man's thing in the early thirties. Perhaps Mother would have tried harder if her driving might not have further stripped Daddy of his masculine pride and confidence. Losing his jobs, not being able to support the family, and now having his wife hired when he wasn't, left him wounded. He did establish a relationship with an insurance agency and tried to sell insurance. But people who could barely keep themselves warm and fed were not likely to buy insurance.

Mother's job was difficult, especially in winter when she had to walk all over the city, calling on people and investigating their eligibility for relief. She came home tired but with some fascinating stories about her clients.

There was a hillbilly family—sorry, Appalachian White—who had a large sprawling clan and lived in a rundown house. Mother never was able to figure out who was married to whom or to which couples the dozen or so children belonged. One day the man who owned the house called the office and said, "Why did you move those people into that old shack of mine? It's not fit for habitation." It turned out they were squatters. There was no place for the family to go so the new landlord fixed the place up a bit and was happy to collect rent through the relief agency. Mother called them her tobacco road family because they reminded her of the family described in the novel *Tobacco Road*.

Then there was the elderly English woman, who had hot tea ready when Mother called. Mother was able to secure permission for her to keep the $100 she had saved for her burial and still get relief dollars. She was so grateful she insisted that she give Mother a blue vase, shaped like a morning glory. Mother broke the rules and took the vase. It is now one of my most precious possessions.

Dad assumed the role of house husband. Every morning, he would cook us a substantial breakfast. Most mornings we would have guests for that meal. Since we lived half a block from the railroad we were a convenient free restaurant for the men who rode the rails in search of work. Most of the town's people handed a sandwich out the door to the tramps but Daddy treated them as guests. He asked them about their families and their travels. I'm sure he had a great deal of sympathy for them because he might well have been one of them, and perhaps his younger brother, Francis, was living that life. I was proud of my Daddy for his compassion.

Mother also fed the tramps when she was at home. She would put Chummy in the dining room, with the door slightly ajar, while the strange men were at her table. She never had to call him to protect her.

Daddy was a better housekeeper than Mother. His Irish mother had had exacting standards. With six children, and only one daughter, her boys all learned to cook, clean and iron. So Daddy washed the clothes, hung them out to dry and ironed. In the thirty five years they were married, Mother never was able to learn to iron a shirt that met his standards, smart woman. He dusted and scrubbed with the best of the women on the street.

He would cook a hearty soup or stew, enough to last several days. We would have had his soup for lunch and when Mother came home from work, tired and drained, she would heat it up for dinner. One time it would be vegetable, another bean soup or perhaps plate boil with potatoes. I loved what Daddy cooked, and if I could get away with it, I'd adopt the same method. Unfortunately my children and my husbands demanded more variety.

Another staple of our diet was corn meal. We would have corn meal for breakfast served as a hot cereal. The leftovers would be poured into a loaf pan to harden. Then at lunch or dinner it would be sliced, fried and served with syrup. We had corn pone often. I suspect that corn meal was inexpensive or perhaps it had been handed out by the government.

In the afternoon, Dad would put on his pressed suit and white shirt and go to try to sell insurance. He also spent a lot of time in the lobby of a hotel in Beaver Falls, visiting with the lawyer who had no clients and the dentist who had no patients. Most evenings we had dinner without him.

With me, he was a warm, nurturing father. I kept my own council and didn't bother my parents with my problems, but I knew that if I decided to confide in Daddy, he would offer a sympathetic ear. Mother was tired and worried much of the time. I'd been in her classroom enough to know how patient she could be. But at home, she used ridicule as a method of discipline— "Flossie, how could you have been so foolish as to...". I knew she loved me and that I could count on her. But if at all possible, I kept my transgressions and problems to myself.

Johnny had difficulty with both parents, but especially with Daddy. John wasn't doing well in school and when Mother tried to help, he ended up crying.

He was only interested in cars, motors and machinery of any kind. He was like an adult in his ability to fix things and figure out how they worked, but his skill wasn't valued in our literate household. He begged to go to Aunt Florey and Uncle John's during vacation, and my tired parents let him. My grandparents reinforced any negative feelings John had about Dad. One phrase that was heard a lot in our house was, "John does the damnedest things!"

I ached for my brother, when he got himself into a fix. I couldn't imagine why he let my parents know about what he did, especially when it was sure to bring punishment. When he did things at school, I often tried to intercede.

What did he do? I remember him taking a frog to school. The teacher thought that was great. When he took a toad, they compared the two. The tadpoles were welcome. But the garter snake caused him to be sent to the principal's office and home for the rest of the day. Shooting up the boy's restroom with a water pistol was another crime.

A few years later when the janitor couldn't fix a thermostat or a typewriter wouldn't work, John was called out of class to fix it. Yet the principal and his teachers thought Johnny had borderline intelligence because he did poorly on a written intelligence test. How could he do well? He couldn't read it. Mother and Dad didn't agree with the results but they seemed powerless to help.

My heart ached for him, even when he did nasty things to me. I understood how hard it must be to be the failing one in a classroom when your little sister led her class.

One time, however, I wasn't so understanding. Johnny had done something to upset me—I don't remember what. I went upstairs into the bedroom and lay on the bed. The room was light and colorful but my mood was dark. I sobbed into mother's flower-garden quilt and blew my nose on the tail of my shirt.

Johnny entered, a look of malicious glee on his face. "Poor little sister, did someone hurt poor little sister and make her cry? Want me to dry your tears, little...."

My foot, clad in leather soled shoes took on a life of its own. It struck like a snake, hitting Johnny square in the face. He looked shocked and then he reddened and tears and blood began to flow. He ran.

I was shocked too. I hadn't thought, just acted. I was guilty. What he had done hadn't deserved that. Besides that, I loved Johnny. We were in this life together. I adored my parents but Johnny and I were both children, and while we experienced life differently, our experiences were more like each others than anyone elses.

Today, almost seventy years later, I still feel a twinge of sorrow when I remember that day. That was the last time I struck my brother.

Chapter 6

Friends and Family

Mother and Dad were acquiring friends in the town. I'm not sure if Daddy's wine-making had anything to do with their popularity, but I'm sure it helped.

We had grapevines in the back yard. Mother made jelly and canned grape juice, but still the vines hung heavy with fruit. She told Dad that he could have the rest to make wine, but he'd have to find money to buy sugar.

Not only did he find money for sugar, but he went out into the woods and picked blackberries, searched the town for unwanted or over ripe fruit and eventually picked dandelions.

The crushed fruit and sugar were put in the cellar in crocks to ferment. One of my fond memories is going to the cellar, lifting the netting, brushing away the fruit flies with a big wooden spoon, and tasting the working wine.

When it was ready, it was put into kegs to age and then bottled and stored in the fruit cellar.

I'm not sure when this activity went on, before or after prohibition. Dad never sold any wine; it was strictly for our use and for entertaining our guests. Some of my classmates were the children of bootleggers. They stood out because their houses and cars were so big and they wore new clothing. It not only would have been illegal to compete with them but dangerous.

Two couples, the Lundees and the Schlingers, visited our home almost every Saturday night. The men would sit in the kitchen and discuss politics and philosophy and the women would sit in the living room and talk about kids, people and ways to make it through this bad time—the important things. I would listen to the both conversations, while making myself inconspicuous in order to avoid bed time commands. Wine was sipped in both rooms.

Eanor Lundee was a Norwegian engineer who had been recruited to work at the car works. He had married Leona Stewart, the daughter of an American engineer. When the layoffs came, he was out of work and the couple and their young baby lived with her parents. With no money for entertainment and no automobile, our house was a welcome Saturday night diversion.

Leona had a first cousin who was an aspiring actor. We followed his career in the papers and through Leona's accounts. When James Stewart starred with Jeanette McDonald and Nelson Eddy in *Rose Marie*, his little fan club in Koppel cheered.

Some years earlier, Wade Stewart, Leona's father changed the climate at the Koppel plant. He had been hired as an engineer and was slated to meet the top management man, a German. He was instructed to walk in and bow slightly, stand at attention, and when the interview was over, back out without turning his back.

Wade, listened to the instructions without comment. He walked in, introduced himself and offered his hand which the surprised manager shook. When the meeting was finished, he said goodbye, turned his back, and walked out.

The man who instructed him was waiting in the outer office and had observed the incident. "Why..?", he asked.

Wade said, "I will treat him just like I would treat the President of the United States or any other man. We don't have royalty here."

Word passed around the plant and the bowing, heel clicking and backing out disappeared.

The Schlingers were Swiss. Max was either working part time or living on money he had saved because things seemed more comfortable at the Schlingers. Ruthie was a few years older than me and was adored by the family who expected great things from her. Maxie was my age and Helen was a few years younger.

Mother and Louise Schlinger spent a lot of time together. Mother taught Louise how to sew and Louise taught Mother how to knit. After a while they abandoned the lessons and Mother sewed for Louise and Louise finished the sweaters Mother had begun.

Max had converted to an eastern religion several years before and the family was vegetarian. Young Maxie ate meat at our house. In fact he ate all the cans of sardines and salmon—both were inexpensive then—that mother had in the pantry. Nothing was said. Dad just made sure it was well supplied for him.

A few years later, when the Roosevelt administration's policies had lessened the depression, our good friends left. The Schlingers went to California where Max had obtained an engineering position and Eanor Lundee found work in New Jersey. They quickly moved into upper-middle class status. It took longer for Koppel and our family to recover from the depression.

Uncle Jack and Aunt Thelma visited. Jack was drinking more and more. Dad told Mother that he poured a water glass full of wine and instead of sipping it, he drank it like water and then asked for a refill. My parents were worried about him.

One night Jack and Dad went to the German Club which was in the American Legion Hall, diagonally across the intersection near our house. They stayed and stayed. Aunt Thelma wanted to get home to relieve the baby-sitter who was with my cousins. Women weren't allowed in the club and both women were sure their men would be upset if they knocked on the door and asked that they be sent home.

It was a summer night. The sisters were dressed in light voile dresses and heels. They stood outside the Club in the grass and wondered what to do. Aunt Thelma said, "Maybe if I just tap on the window with my shoe, Jack will hear it and know it is me." The window was a basement window, at ground level. Auntie tapped. But she lost her balance and her foot went through, sending glass crashing down on the tables.

She and Mother ran as fast as their heels permitted and disappeared into the summer night. The men rushed up the stairs and wondered what prohibitionist had attacked their domain. Uncle Jack and Daddy knew who had broken the window — but they never told.

A few years later, Uncle Jack had lost his job and his home. He was severely depressed and admitted to a mental hospital. He did recover and managed to earn a living as a produce manager in the grocery store where he began his career. But Aunt Thelma never again joined a country club.

One time Mother came home from work and heard a noise in the basement. She opened the door and there was the water meter reader. He had arrived that morning and found the wine cellar. He was too drunk to climb the stairs. Mother put a chair under the door handle when she closed it, to keep him out of the kitchen. Then she sent Johnny to find Daddy.

When Dad arrived he helped the poor fellow up the stairs and took him home. We lived in Koppel for seven more years, and never received a water bill.

My parents were well known in the town, especially Mother. I was welcome in all the homes, especially the families with Italian names. I liked their open hospitality and the noisy exchanges between family members.

Mr. Bartett's rooster became a problem when I was in second grade. He chased me. Some days, I was afraid to go past him to go home for lunch, and stood hesitating until the school bell rang for afternoon classes. Finally, I decided to outbluff him. I lost. He got me down in a ditch and was pecking and scratching me. Mrs. DeSanzo heard my screams and rescued me from that ferocious bird. After she took me home, she marched down to the Bartetts with a demand. Mr. Bartett took care of the problem and that night delivered a nicely dressed and plucked chicken to our house, all ready for the pot.

There were no orchestras or bands at our school. But the first and second grades had a rhythm band. The teachers put a record on the scratchy old victrola and we children kept time to it. I played the sticks. I sat on the floor with a line of stick-players, hit my two sticks on the floor or on each other, according to the accent of the beat. I envied the lucky kids who got to play the cymbals or bells.

A program was scheduled at the Methodist Church for the Rhythm Band and other entertainment by the students of the school. Daddy got out my favorite dress, a yellow taffeta creation with ruffles. He called it my butterfly dress. I loved it and wearing it was a treat. My parents and all the other parents were there when we performed. Cookies and punch were served afterwards. Someone mentioned the music the Rhythm Band had accompanied, and Daddy announced that it was the Anvil Chorus from the opera *Il Trovatore*. Even though I detected a few eyes rolled skyward, I was proud of my Daddy.

Second grade passed without any major disruption. I do remember looking at the alphabet that was posted above the blackboard and thinking that I should learn it. Oh, I did know the letters and sounds but I didn't know which came first. I had taught myself to read by sight and had deduced enough about the sounds to figure out the words. I did finally learn my ABCs but not very well. Years later working in a doctor's office, my employer watched me search the files for a record and teased me about not knowing the order of the letters. I considered this a trivial handicap since I didn't plan to do much filing.

Johnny broke my last doll. He also ruined my baby stroller by trying to ride in it. I found a milk bottle with a rounded top, fashioned to hold the cream separate from the milk, put a bonnet on it, wrapped it in a piece of blanket, and had a doll.

Damond's pond was a source of pleasure for the town's children. It was at the end of our block. It was a shallow pond about half an acre in size, beside the railroad tracks. When I stood in it the water came up to my waist. Frogs, tadpoles and leeches abounded in the murky water. I'm sure it was polluted with every germ in town. And yet we paddled around there in the summer, stopping occasionally to pull the leeches off. All the town's children, except perhaps the German children played in the pond. No one seemed to be concerned about where we were and there were no adults present.

In the wintertime, we played on the ice at the

pond. Only a few of the children had skates, probably passed down from an older sibling who received them at a more prosperous time. But we slid around on the ice and had fun.

When it snowed and packed the streets we sledded on the hills. John and I did have sleds. The cars slowed or stopped for us. I do remember running into a fireplug and getting a bloody nose, and a parked car's running board and cutting my lip. Again, there were no adults present and we children amused ourselves, and took care of our bruises.

There was a dome shaped hill, across the main highway that went by the town. It was known as the knob. It was great fun in winter. You didn't need a sled; a piece of tin would do to send you hurtling down the slope.

The world was much less child centered than it is now. The adults were struggling to survive and if children were fed and sheltered, that was almost enough. It meant we had a great deal of freedom, to roam the town and play at will.

Johnny and I got the whooping cough. We were quarantined and a big sign was placed on our house. After the initial onslaught of the illness, we felt fine and played outside in the yard. However we had a problem when we coughed, which was often—we vomited. My parents solved the problem by equipping each of us with an empty coffee can, complete with a string that went around our necks. When we stopped to cough, we grabbed our can. What I remember most vividly was being hungry. I would be so starved and eat with gusto. But if I began to cough, up came the meal, and I would have to eat all over again. When we made the visits to the grandparents, Dad would stop the car so we could empty our cans at the side of the road.

Young babies often died of whooping cough. My mother had acquired it as a young teacher. At first it was believed that she had tuberculosis. The man to whom she was engaged fled from her in fear. It was finally correctly diagnosed and she spent a summer on the farm recovering. When her former fiancee tried to see her and reinstate the relationship, she refused him.

As a child I heard stories about how diphtheria decimated my parents' generation. Aunt Thelma struggled all her life with the illness she first acquired as a complication from diphtheria. Her little brother had died and nearly every family of that generation had lost a child to diphtheria. Even as a child, I had great respect for preventive immunizations.

My natural grandparents, Grandma and Grandpa Tom, sold the farm in Princeton and moved to a small farm near my adopted grandparents. Grandpa struck his hand with a hammer when he was working in the barn. At first it seemed like a small injury, but then it became infected. There were no antibiotics at that time. The infection spread and in order to save his life, they amputated his hand. The infection still raged and little by little they amputated until they reached a spot a few inches below his shoulder. His arm and the infection were eliminated, but he was alive.

Grandpa continued to keep his small farm productive. He found ingenious ways to wheel a wheelbarrow, mow the lawn and shoot a gun. He could milk a cow almost as fast with one hand as most people did with two. His garden flourished, and the wood was piled high for Grandma's cook stove every fall.

In my career as a nurse, I have given thousands of penicillin injections. And when I've had a moment on the busy ward to reflect, I thanked God and Alexander Fleming for that life saving substance.

Shortly after we moved to Koppel we joined the Methodist Church. Mother had always been a Methodist. Dad had been raised Catholic and had been devout in his youth. But he had left the Church when he married Mother. Johnny and I attended Sunday school. One Sunday I had attended church alone and they were having baptisms. So I joined the crowd of children and was baptized.

When Daddy and Mother were there, we always discussed the sermon on the way home. Dad usually dissected it critically. It seemed strange to me that he and the minister seemed to enjoy talking to each other so much and discussing the same topics as the sermons. As I got older, I realized that for Daddy, criticism and arguing were sport.

Daddy also enjoyed talking with priests when he chanced to meet one. In the small top dresser drawer where he kept his shirt studs and cuff links there were religious medals and mass cards.

I often went off to mass with my friend, Anna Mangeri. When Mother was invited for a wedding at the Catholic Church I was happy to go along. I loved the mystery and beauty of the Catholic ceremony, with its Latin responses.

Years later, when Mother was an old woman in a nursing home, I was planning to move from upstate New York to Oregon. I talked with her and told her I was willing to take her with me, or she could stay where she was, close to Johnny and my daughter, Shevawn. She decided to come with me.

On a visit to Oregon, I found a good nursing home run by Catholic sisters, and reserved a space for Mother. When I told her she said, "Oh good, I think I'll convert. Your Dad always wanted me to. He wanted us to get married again in the Church. I could have after Aunt Florey and Uncle John died. If I'd done it before they'd have disinherited me. But I felt that I was already married and to go through another ceremony...Well, anyway, he'd be happy to know I finally did it."

The elderly nun who instructed Mother said that she had never known anyone who learned so quickly. What Sister didn't know was that the doctrines weren't so very different, and Mother had learned the Methodist doctrine well.

When Mother died, I didn't know what to do. Her funeral would be in Pennsylvania, where the family graves were and where she had continued to support the Methodist Church. The former priest who lived next door solved the problem for me.

"Florence, take her home to Pennsylvania and have a Methodist funeral. When you come back, have a mass said for her at the nursing home. Joanne and I will come and be with you."

And that is what I did.

Chapter 7

Learning to Survive and Life in the Apartment

Third grade was memorable because it was the only time I was punished physically in school. Miss Ray was my teacher. She was a thin nervous woman about forty who had a perpetual worried expression. I was still the quiet, shy little girl who did my work and had little to say, not the sort of student one would expect to be punished.

It was music class and we were singing from old dog-eared books. Most of the corners of the pages were turned down. Without thinking I tore a corner off and put it in my mouth. Miss Ray saw me and told me not to do that. I nodded yes and kept on singing.

A few songs later, she called, "Flossie!" and I realized that I had been doing it again. She commanded that I come to the front of the room and hold out my hands. She held them tightly and paddled them with a ruler.

In addition to the humiliation, it hurt like hell! Daddy's razor strap applied to the posterior had been far less painful. I cried and cried— eyes and nose pouring out tears and mucous. And Miss Ray continued to beat my small palms.

Then blood spurted out of my nose and all over her clean blouse. The beating stopped and she began to try to stanch the flow. I continued to cry and bleed. I could see that she was frightened so I cried louder, now in anger.

That was the last time I received physical punishment in school. I bet Miss Ray retired that cursed ruler. I hoped that she would never get my blood out of her clothing.

Daddy was mad when I told him. Mother, who had paddled a child or two in her years as a teacher, was more understanding of Miss Ray's frustration. A third grader who eats a book must be stopped.

Things were not going well with Mother's work. The male supervisor played favorites among the investigators and there may have been some sexual harassment going on. Strict guidelines about the amount of money allocated to the families were sometimes violated. Mother unburdened herself to Dad when she came home at night. I listened and worried.

Daddy had a trait that made me cringe inside, even as a child. If someone hurt or insulted him or anyone in our family, he got even. He would wait and watch and when the person transgressed, he'd make sure they were punished. He never did anything directly to hurt them, but let them hang themselves and then made sure someone in charge knew what had happened. The malicious joy he felt in getting them made me ashamed of my beloved Daddy.

He waited, watched mother's supervisor, and finally wrote a few letters. When the man was fired, he rejoiced. I resolved never to tell him if anyone hurt me.

Our possessions continued to be sold, even after Mother had a job. Somehow her salary was never enough. Daddy needed dental care and he traded his Harvard Classics for care for the entire family. Six decades later, when I smile, I sometimes think of Daddy with gratitude.

My parents fought, not often, perhaps twice a year. Once I remember they had a terrible quarrel because Dad wanted to hang the washing outside on a Sunday. Mother objected saying that the neighbors would see. Dad said, "To hell with the neighbors!", and the fight began.

It ended in the standard way. Dad would say, "I'm going to get out of this God Damn place!" Then he'd throw some clothes into a suitcase and leave in the car.

The house would be still and sad. I remember feeling as if my heart would break and it hurt to breathe.

In a little while, the time varied depending on the intensity of the quarrel, Dad would return. Sometimes he'd smell a little of beer but he was never drunk. He'd have a present for Mother—jewelry, nice soap, perfume. She'd still be mad, but resigned and they would make up. She would occasionally reject the gifts, which she would eventually have to pay for, and he frequently gave them to me.

Mother's position in these family arguments was one I agreed with. But I loved my Daddy and my heart ached when I saw him hurt and contrite.

The Works Progress Administration, a part of President Franklin Roosevelt's plan for recovery, came into being and the town lost its air of disappointment. Things began to happen. Suddenly the streets were filled with the men of the town who broke rock and paved them.

One rock breaker was of particular interest to the town's people. Betty Jean Little's father, Frank Little, had been a boss at the plant. Evidently he was unpopular with the men. Then when the depression had first begun, he was in charge of distributing food. Among the food was milk. He learned that some of the families had made ice cream with the milk they were given and refused to give them milk on the next distribution day. Apparently Mr. Little believed charity shouldn't be enjoyed.

Some of the men who had worked for him made it a point to go to the street where he was wielding a shovel in preparation for paving the street. They stood and watched. Mr. Little ignored them.

Years later, when the depression was over, Mother saw Mrs. Little in a department store in Pittsburgh. She was wearing a fur coat and looked very prosperous. Mother spoke to her by name. The woman looked at her coldly and turned away.

When Mother told me about seeing Mrs.Little, I was grateful that our family hadn't been ashamed of being poor. We felt that it was something that could happen to anyone.

There was a park about half mile from the town. The swimming pool, bath houses and outside dance floor had been abandoned. Men from the WPA repaired them, supplied playground equipment, and two unemployed teachers were hired to begin a summer recreation program.

Johnny and I spent many happy hours in the pool. I learned to swim. In the evening we'd sit beside the dance floor, listening to the *"Rippling rhythm"* of Shep Fields and his orchestra and watching the adults dance.

Mother left her job as a relief investigator and was hired as the supervisor of the WPA sewing room. It was located in one of the temporary school buildings behind our house. The single women of the town, the widows, divorced or never married, were employed there making clothes to dress the inhabitants.

Mother's ladies made clothes for all ages and sexes. Soon all of my classmates were clad in Mother's designs made from government supplied print cloth. The boys would wear the shirts she designed and the girls would wear dresses in a familiar print. Since she was the supervisor and supposedly made enough money to clothe us, we did not receive an allotment of clothing. But if you had lifted up my skirt you would have found WPA underclothing and at night I slept in WPA pajamas.

I was proud of my Mother. She was so slim and pretty—and clever too. My friends' mothers were dowdy compared to her. One time she got some bright print material—not government supplied—and made herself beach pajamas. Slacks had not yet become common and these pajamas with wide legs were their forerunner. Word spread through the town that Mrs. Fisher was wearing beach pajamas and several women came calling to see the latest fashion.

I needed a winter coat. She took her own warm coat and remade it into a coat for me. Since she then had no warm coat, she wore a rain coat with a sweater under it. I never doubted that my mother loved me.

In fourth grade it suddenly became apparent that that quiet little Fisher girl was pretty smart. When we studied Geography and History, I was able to add a lot to the lessons, because I was reading so much. One time the teacher asked us what we wanted to be when we grew up. When my turn came I said, "An opera singer."

The teacher looked shocked and said, "What?" and I repeated my answer.

Too bad that in spite of my love for music, I had a terrible voice. Another time, when we were singing I stuck up my hand and said, "The tune to this song is La donna e mobile from *Rigoletto* by Verdi". There was shocked silence—and I suspect that my classmates eyes were rolled skyward. The teacher recovered herself and agreed.

Smart kid that I was, I became aware that it was difficult to be the smartest kid in the class—now called the class nerd—and be popular. I did some soul searching about this and finally decided that it was more important to me to be true to myself than to be popular. I was so grateful that I didn't have the learning problems my brother struggled with, that I felt I had an obligation to use my talents. Besides, learning new things about the world was fun. I've never been sorry that I made that decision.

I had a chronic sore throat from fourth grade until my tonsils were removed when I was a high school junior. I missed a lot of school but I didn't mind, I stayed home and read. Mother didn't seem concerned about my absences and I continued to lead the class.

The family moved from the yellow house to an apartment over the hardware store. I don't know why. Perhaps we were evicted. Just before we moved, Mother sold our drop leaf dining room table. It must have paid the rent deposit. Dad stripped the horrid green paint off the kitchen table, sanded it and stained it maple. It looked great.

As I remember it, we just picked up our furniture, walked down by the Legion Hall, crossed the tracks and passed by Bartetts. Then we walked down a block, through a vacant lot, and up the twenty two steps into a hall that led to our new home.

Surely there must have been a truck or car involved at some point. However all I remember are scenes such as Daddy carrying the head board of the bed and Mother and Johnny tagging behind with the bed slats.

Our new apartment was at the back of the building and looked out over the roof of the store's garage. Originally it had been planned as a four room apartment, living and dining rooms, kitchen and bath and one bedroom. However the building's owner, who was the hardware merchant, had rented it to his daughter, a nurse. She had six children after moving there, and at some point, an extra room was added. The room had almost as much square footage as the rest of the apartment. We heard that she had put six beds in it and called it the ward. I shared the ward with Johnny. We had plenty of space for our beds, toys and all the extras that a household collects.

One of the windows in the living room was actually a glass door. There were two steps under it and it led to a large porch, resting on top of the garage roof. Window boxes surrounded the porch and we planted morning glories in them. The vines partially shielded the porch from view. It was almost as though we had a lawn, a tar paper one. In fact, Johnny and I crawled out of the ward's window onto the roof regularly. One time we even did it when the roof was covered with snow, in our bare feet.

We had a new large radio that stood in the place of honor between two living room windows. On Sundays we ate in the dining room and even had wine with dinner. The rest of the days we crowded around a small porcelain topped table in the kitchen.

Johnny was eleven and I was nine when we moved to the apartment. Dad was away more selling, or trying to sell, insurance, and Mother was busy with her job. We children were on our own.

One summer day Mother came home for lunch

and informed us that she would be bringing her boss to the apartment for a discussion. They needed to talk about some things away from the sewing room.

She said, "John, you are a mess. You'll have to clean yourself up. I'd be ashamed if my supervisor saw you."

"Don't worry, Mom," my brother replied, "I won't embarrass you."

Several hours later, Mother was walking down the street with her superior. A very dirty boy approached, looked up at her and said, "Hello, Mrs. Fisher."

Mother, almost bursting with laughter, controlled herself and replied, "Hello, John."Then she passed on by.

Mother developed a reputation among the WPA administrators as a person who could handle problem employees. There was one woman who lived and worked in the WPA sewing room in Elwood City, across the river from Koppel, who frightened her supervisor. Mother was asked if she would take her and she agreed.

Mrs. Washington arrived ten minutes before the sewing room opened. She was a small black woman whose face was fixed in a rigid scowl. Mother introduced herself and showed her where she might hang her coat. Then she asked which tasks she liked to do and assigned her to one of them. When the other women arrived, Mother introduced them, being sure to use their titles, Miss or Mrs.

Mrs. Washington pedaled away furiously for several days and then her face softened and the scowl vanished. Mother continued to use her title and made liberal use of the lubricants of human relations, the words 'please' and 'thank you'.

After a month, Mother's supervisor stopped by. She approached Mrs. Washington and asked how things were going. Mrs. Washington replied in emphatic tones, "Mrs. Fisher is a lady".

Mother reported this to the family that night at dinner. I was very proud of my mother and hoped that I would follow her and treat everyone with respect.

Some of the things that Johnny and I did would have frightened our parents if they had known about them. John, on a dare, swam the Beaver River on a Good Friday. Fortunately he lived up to his reputation as a strong swimmer.

My friend, Anna Mangeri, and I played in the railroad yard along the river. One time we were under a railroad car that looked as though it were abandoned and had been there a long time. We were recovering from a battle with the nettles plants that grew along the river. All of a sudden the car began to roll. I bolted out from under it and ran up a bank. I was afraid to look behind me to see what had happened to Anna. Then to my great relief, I heard her beside me.

Another time, Anna and I were walking down the road toward the park. A man drove by, then stopped and called to us. He asked us if we knew where a certain woman lived. We didn't know her and told him. Then he said, "She likes to f___ a lot." We couldn't believe our ears— actually. A grown-up saying that word! Surely we had heard wrong.

The man turned the car around and came back.

He stopped again. I was close enough to look in the car. He had unzipped his pants and was displaying the biggest, reddest *thing*. It was enormous. I'd seen my brothers and my younger cousin's *little things*, but this....Anna and I raced into the woods and he drove on. Then we each went to our homes. I crawled under my bed and curled up in the dust. I felt guilty. I never told my parents.

One summer day, Mother took me with her when she called on one of the women who worked at the sewing room, Mrs. Warren. She was a lady in her fifties, a widow who lived with her daughter, Elizabeth. Elizabeth was in her thirties and crippled by polio. She had worked at the sewing room also, doing buttonholes and hand work, but evidently steady work was too difficult with her physical problems and she no longer worked. She was a pleasant redheaded woman. When we left she invited me to visit.

I took her invitation seriously and soon I was there almost every day. We read together. She had saved the magazines that had serialized *Rebecca*, and we thrilled to that gothic romance. We read *Thelma*, the book that had inspired my grandmother to call my aunt by that name. Mrs. Warren seemed upset that I was there so much. I'm sure Elizabeth was lonely and had no friends her age. I spent several summers visiting Elizabeth and then found other things to do.

As an adult, I've looked back on that time with Elizabeth and am sorry I never let her know how much her friendship meant to me.

Johnny and I got the measles and stayed home

from school. Mother had to go to work and Dad had an appointment so we were alone. I was in my parents' bed in the bedroom and John was bedded down in the ward. We were both too sick to read, socialize or listen to the radio. As the day began to darken, I began to watch the clock, counting off the time until Mother came home.

Suddenly Johnny began to scream. I sat up in bed startled. Then he dashed into the living room, naked, screaming about the man that was trying to make him swallow burning string. I got out of bed and tried to calm him. His skin burned under my touch.

Then I heard Mother's key in the lock. I almost cried with relief. She examined John and even before she took off her coat, ran a tepid bath for him. Soon his fever was under control. In a few days, we were well.

Johnny spent time during the summer at Grandpa John's. I visited Grandpa Tom's. I was aware that Grandma Tom liked me but she never made any overtly affectionate gestures. Grandpa Tom called me pet names and spoke to me with warmth. Of course he had named a pig Flossie. But I didn't mind since the other pigs bore the names of his other grandchildren. I was expected to do chores but there was plenty of time to play.

A family moved a travel trailer into the woods across the road from Grandpa's. The man was a structural iron worker, working on a project in New Castle. They were there several summers. The family was Mohawk Indian. Their niece, Dulcie White, who was my age lived with them and we became friends.

Dulcie and I roamed the fields and woods together. She told me all about the ceremonies of her tribe and I was enthralled with her stories. When the summers were over and the building was finished, the family left and I lost a good friend.

About this time, I became, mother's confidante. She began to talk to me about her distress with Daddy. She worked hard at her job, paid the bills and was the responsible adult. He spent more money driving around and trying or pretending to sell insurance than he made. It seemed that appearing to be a successful gentleman was more important than actually earning a living. She talked about leaving Dad. She and I would live together. Johnny would go to live with Aunt Florey and Uncle John.

Perhaps she felt she was preparing me for what might happen, or just using me as a sounding board. But I suffered with the knowledge. I felt guilty when I was with Daddy for having listened to her talk about him, at the same time, I sympathized with her situation.

Years later, after Daddy died and we were both mature women, she told me about the deep romantic love and fantastic sex that bonded her and Daddy. When she was an elderly widow and a man showed interest in her she turned him down, telling me when I asked why, "I had the best. After your Dad, other men just wouldn't measure up."

When I was a student nurse in New York City, Daddy came to the city on business and visited me. We went sightseeing and to plays. I had a wonderful time. All the time, however, he was talking about

Mother and wishing that she were with us. We even concocted amusing little stories to tease her with and he saved all the programs and menus. He was a man very much in love with his wife.

As an adult, I have looked back and wished that I could have had a clearer picture of my parents' marriage than I did as a frightened nine year old. Perhaps parents should be more open about their relationships. Then again, at nine or any age before twenty, I might not have understood what goes on between a man and a woman.

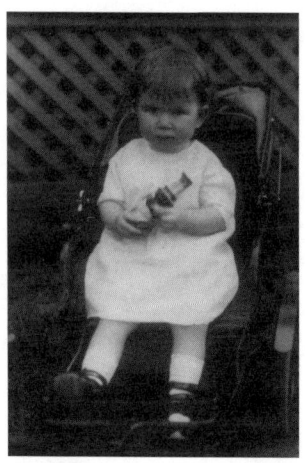

Florence Alice Fisher, 1928

"Flossie" is on the pillow. Florence Baird, Grandma John, is leading brother John Fisher away, 1927

Thomas Baird and Alice Marshall Baird Grandma & Grandpa Tom, 1940

My parents, Floray Baird Fisher and Joseph L. Fisher, 1933

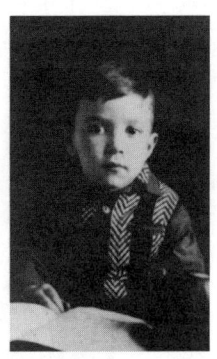

My Grandfathers, Brother John Baird (seated) and Thomas Baird, about 1900

John Fisher " Johnny" 1931

Fifth Grade Class, Koppel, Pennsylvania, 1936 Flossie is in the front row wearing a dark skirt and sweater, which had been hastily removed from the dirty clothes hamper that morning.

Friends—Edys Hayes, Flossie Fisher, and Virginia Lee Stump, in front of North Beaver Twp. High School, Mt. Jackson, Pa. 1943

The Prom. The boys were all in the army.

On the way to the Senior Prom, 1944.
Florence Fisher, Virginia Lee Stump, Vera Olson,
Edys Hayes and Mary Henry

Pvt. John Fisher
Combat Engineer, 1943

Seaman Donald Hardesty
" My Sailor, 1943"

John and Thelma Lusk, Aunt Thelma and Uncle Jack, and sons Cpl. William Lusk, Army Air Force Medic, and Petty Officer John Lusk, Navy Submarine Service, 1943

Florence Fisher,
High School Graduation
1944

Friend Eleanor
Hoffmaster,
1945

Florence Fisher
US Cadet Nurse Corps, 1944

Envelope of letter to
Florence Fisher from her Father.

Letter to Florence Fisher from her Father

1-9-45

Hello, sweetheart:—

We received your letter. Sorry there were not enough boys at party. But glad that you and the kids celebrated afterward.

Mother is back in the harness again. While at home she spends her time on Davenport, surrounded with books — I help her with English and History.

I ruined the motor of my car in a snow drift the other day. They tried to get me a new motor, but can't. I think they can fix it alright. A connecting rod went thro' the Block — They are going to sleeve the cylinder wall.

Rather than give so much to phone Co., we will not call you so much. Then we can keep you in more money. We can write. It doesn't cost so much.

Don't say anything to anybody about this! — We think John D. McBrate was wounded in France. Isn't that too bad? Remember! "To noone".

We have not heard from John, nor has Marjorie.

The weather here is bad. The mailman said it is the worse he has ever seen — He has been on this route for 26 years.

I sent your clothes — Let us know when you receive them.

Well, be a good girl, and let us know if you want anything. Dad

Chapter 8

Being Blackmailed, Visiting Relatives and Entertainment

Johnny was busy with his friends and boy interests. We had almost stopped playing with each other. The nightly reading had ceased. It was more fun for me to read silently and John no longer seemed interested. Although the ward was a huge room and we did try to make a partial partition with orange crates, I longed for my own private space.

Anna Mangeri and I were curious about sex, this forbidden topic that only adults knew about. One time when we played house in the woods, we simulated the sex act. It wasn't as though we were attracted to each other. We were just playing around.

Somehow Johnny saw or heard about this episode. He threatened to tell my parents. When he taunted me about it, my insides would crawl with shame. This went on for weeks. Since we shared a room, there was no way I could escape him. Sometimes Glen Marshall would be with him. I liked Glen and would have liked to consider him a boy friend. His being with Johnny when he tortured me only added to the humiliation.

I began to hide from my oppressor. When I would hear him coming up the stairs, I would lift the lid of the cedar chest and crawl inside. If Glen were with him, I would listen, hoping to learn information that I could use to defend myself.

Finally, Mother noticed that I was acting strange and mentioned it to Johnny. The dirty rat told her about Anna and me. How I hated him!

Mother had a little talk with me. It was a relief not to be blackmailed. But I hated Johnny.

When I had my own children there was a strict rule against blackmail in our household.

The hate died and the warm feelings toward my brother eventually did return and deepen. In our later childhood and all the rest of our lives we loved and supported each other. Our relation was the longest close relationship I've had, seventy years. I was with Johnny when he died.

At least twice a year Mother and Daddy took us to Pittsburgh. In the winter we'd see the Christmas parade and shop in the big department stores. When Mother wanted to do some shopping on her own, she left us in the toy department. Another child care substitute was the escalator. She'd leave us at one and we'd ride up and down. When she had finished she'd return to the moving steps and soon we'd appear. No one, except perhaps the store employees, thought this arrangement was improper.

We'd visit the museums and spend a day looking and learning. Both Johnny and I liked the Egyptian exhibits with the mummies. On another trip we would spend the day at the Zoo. We especially liked the big cats and the primates. Johnny, always had to spend some time in the reptile house.

Although some of my classmates were more affluent than our family, we were the only children whose parents made sure they had such experiences. In many ways our young years were rich.

John and I still had occasional adventures together. One Fall day Dad and I visited a retired physician, Dr. Doyle. He lived about two miles from us, up the highway and down a long lane. His house was a very old stone house. I suspect that it was the oldest building in the area. I don't remember what business had taken Daddy there, but soon we were in the house, being treated like honored guests. Dr. Doyle showed Dad the features of the house, the huge fireplace, the thick walls that allowed for window seats and the walnut paneling. The old gentleman told stories about the early settlers and showed us Native American artifacts. I had a wonderful time.

I told Johnny about the visit and he was disappointed that he hadn't been along. He persuaded me to take him there. I was a little reluctant, but was tempted by the idea of repeating a wonderful experience. I said that I would.

The weather had changed; winter had arrived. Dressed in winter coats, scarves and galoshes we trudged up the highway. When we got to the lane, that curved up along a ravine, Johnny suggested that we take a short cut. I was afraid that the low spot he wanted to cross would be a swamp, but he convinced me that if it were, it would be frozen.

We started through the swale, avoiding the bushes and brambles that grew there. It soon became evident that it was a swamp, and even though the road was frozen, the ice we attempted to walk across would not hold us. By the time we reached the lane and stood in front of the house, we were a wet, miserable pair.

Suddenly I was afflicted with a severe attack of shyness. How could I go up to the door and announce to the old gentleman, that we two had come to visit? I couldn't be persuaded. Johnny was furious. He marched resolutely back down the lane with me trailing behind, muttering apologies and explanations. He was mad at me for several days. Big brothers can be mean, but little sisters are sometimes a pain in the neck.

Our lives were enriched by my parents' extended families. We visited Mother's parents, both sets of them, almost every week. Grandpa Tom was the only grandparent who was overtly affectionate but I knew that Grandma Tom and Grandpa John loved me. Grandma John didn't like me but what she felt had ceased to matter. I was always polite to her, however. As I grew a little older, I began to sense her terrible loneliness and isolation.

Aunt Thelma and her boys had moved into an apartment in a house that her parents owned. It was next door to their home. The rest of the large farmhouse was occupied by mother's brother Bill, his wife

Edna, and their two boys. Uncle Jack was still away in the mental hospital. There were lots of cousins to play with when we visited Grandma and Grandpa Tom.

Vacations were spent visiting relatives. Dad's older brother, Peter Jerome Fisher, lived in Coaldale, Pennsylvania, the town where Dad was born. It was in the anthracite region of the state but the mines were no longer working.

Uncle Pete was a music teacher. He taught piano and played organ for the local Catholic church. He was much older than Daddy and his son Liam was almost Dad's age. He also had a daughter, Mary.

We visited once when I was five or six. Uncle Pete had stopped playing the piano a few years before. It seemed that he was inclined to linger too long at the local bar on Sunday morning and be late getting to the church to play for mass. One morning he arrived to hear music streaming out the church door. His best student had taken his place. Uncle Pete then stopped going to church and dropped his teaching. In the summer he would sit on the porch and greet all the people who passed by on the way to mass.

Dad persuaded him to break his vow of not touching the piano and we were treated to a concert of classic piano compositions. It seemed as though the whole town was smiling because Pete Fisher was playing again.

Uncle Pete's wife, Cecilia or Aunt Celie, had an Irish brogue. One evening, Pete played Irish jigs and she climbed up on the kitchen table and danced for us.

Cousin Liam had two children whose names I've forgotten. There was a girl about my age who entertained us with a tap dance. Mother and Dad had no childish entertainment to offer. But not to worry, Little Flossie stepped up to the center of the room and recited Edward Lear's *The Owl and the Pussycat*, followed by Eugene Field's touching poem, *Little Boy Blue*. I could have, but refrained from, doing *Inviticus* or *Thanatopsis*. I was afraid they'd ask me what they meant and I wasn't sure. My parents' faces glowed with pride.

We toured the coal mines where my Grandfather and Daddy had worked. One tunnel, a mile long, under a mountain was named for my Grandfather. He had been an orphan who immigrated with his brother from Ireland when they were twelve and fourteen. Somehow, before he left Ireland, my Grandfather had acquired a good education in literature, music and mathematics. He drew up the plans for the tunnel and they began digging at both ends. When they met in the middle, his calculations were off only an inch.

Uncle Pete died not long after we visited and we never returned to Coaldale. I've had no contact with his children.

Aunt Mame, Mary Veronica, was Dad's only sister. She too was older than he and her oldest son was only a few years younger than Dad. She lived in Millville, New Jersey, was divorced and had four sons. We visited her several times. Atlantic City and Ocean City were about twenty miles from her place so

Johnny and I swam in the Atlantic, built sand castles on the shore and ate our fill of salt water taffy. We were exposed to the wonders of the Steel Pier at Atlantic City, a 1930's version of Las Vegas but without the gambling. Johnny and Dad went fishing and Johnny hooked a small shark. We ate it with relish. All that was required for these visits was enough gas to get us there and a little spending money.

Aunt Mame and her son Jerome visited us almost every summer. Jerry was unmarried and a devoted son. He drove his mother to Koppel. I remember walking down the street one day with my handsome blond cousin. I told him that I was nine and he confessed that he was thirty-one, twenty-two years older than me. I looked up at him and thought, he's an old man!

Jerry married during WII and had a nice family. All through the years in times of family crisis, Jerry would come. At my father's funeral, Jerry wrapped the rosary he had carried all through the battles of the South Pacific, around Dad's hand. It was comforting to know that Dad, who had a strong emotional bond to the Catholic Church even though he was a nominal Methodist, was buried with a tangible token of his faith. The last time I saw Jerry was at my Mother's funeral. He died several years ago.

Dad's youngest brother was Francis. Aunt Mame and Dad spent a lot of time discussing him. Mame said he always arrived at her place, unannounced, at night, wearing sun glasses. The conclusion was that he was in some sort of trouble.

He had been married and had two little girls. Mother and Daddy talked a lot about Betty and Janie. Then Janie died and the marriage broke up. Where Francis was and what he was doing was a mystery.

One night there was a knock on the door and there was a man in sunglasses. It was Uncle Francis. He stayed a few days. I don't remember much about him but he seemed to be a pleasant man. Dad warned me not to talk about him.

A week later, I was sitting on a bench outside the hardware store. A tall man in a suit approached and asked my name. I told him and then he asked if my Uncle Frank had been to visit.

I replied, "I know I have an Uncle Francis, but I don't remember him. I've heard my parents talk about him."

He tried a few more questions but I stuck to my story.

Then he went upstairs to talk with Daddy. Daddy said, "Yes, his brother Francis had been there, but he didn't know where he was now."

Then Dad asked to see a picture of the Frank Fisher they were looking for. It was not a picture of his brother, at least that is what he told the man.

I thought I did a pretty good job of lying to the investigator but I was worried that I might be in trouble. I was relieved when my parents said that no one would bother a nine year old who lied to a cop—especially to protect an uncle.

Years later, when my brother was in the Army in Texas, Uncle Francis came to visit him. He was married and very religious. Johnny had the impression that he had been in prison for a long time.

We saw Dad's brother, Jim, more than Dad's other relatives. I remember vividly the time he brought my cousin, thirteen-year-old Mickey, to stay with us. They arrived in a Model A Ford sedan. The back seat was packed to the roof with their belongings. Mickey's things were carried up the steps to the ward and he settled in there. Even as a child, I felt the sadness about the situation. Everything they owned was in the back of that car.

Mickey was a pleasant, handsome boy with dark eyes and hair. He looked like my father. I don't know how long he stayed. One of his prize possessions was a model of a ship. When Uncle Jim finally came back for him, he took it with him.

He did leave a book behind however, a leather bound volume of the works of Guy de Maupasant. It was a beautiful book. It stayed in my parents' library for years and later was in mine. I read and enjoyed the stories, but I always had the nagging feeling that I had it because of Mickey's misfortune. Fifty years later, Mickey and his wife visited me in Portland and I returned his book.

In the fall of 1936 I took part in my first presidential campaign. The children of the town were recruited to parade through the streets carrying signs urging the re-election of President Franklin Roosevelt. I don't know why they bothered: there was never any doubt that he would be re-elected. Everyone in the town loved the President. He had saved the banks, put people back to work with his programs and kept the country from ruin. When he had one of his fireside chats, we all were glued to our radios.

Through the cold fall evening, I dutifully carried a sign that read, "Landon and Knox, Fall on the Rocks!" and was rewarded with a candy bar. FDR was reelected by a landslide.

On Sundays we made our usual trip to see the Grandparents. Usually this meant grinding through a muddy country road for the last three miles to Grandpa John's house. Sometime after 1936, we sped along a macadam highway. The WPA had paved the road.

On another Sunday we found Grandpa John in bed, gravely ill with pneumonia. He had been sick more than a week but Aunt Florey hadn't called us. Mother summoned the doctor and made arrangements for us to stay. The next day, I was playing outside in the fallen leaves, when Mother called me in and told me that Grandpa had died.

Mother and Daddy helped Aunt Florey with the funeral arrangements and later, with the lawyers. Grandpa had left a very strange will. Evidently he believed that Aunt Florey would die first. Although she had jointly owned everything and owned it solely after Grandpa died, the will said that everything was to be sold and placed in trust for mother. In part this may have been done to make sure that Dad didn't get control of the money. That wasn't legal in the circumstances. So the will was bypassed and Aunt Florey made a new one leaving her property to Mother.

Mother worried about Aunt Florey being alone in a country house. Johnny spent summers and vacations with her. He wanted to be there but I'm not sure it was good for him. Mother arranged for a neighbor woman to do the heavy work and stop in daily. But antiques and other valuables disappeared from the house and no one seemed to know if they had been given away or stolen. Aunt Florey spent her days sitting in a large rocking chair in the living room, rocking and engaged in dialogue with people who were not present.

In Koppel a new diversion had arrived. The deserted theater beside the hardware store was renovated. It had a musty odor and the seats felt damp, but who worried about such things when enchantment was offered on the screen. It cost ten cents to get in and once inside, you could stay as long as you liked. There was one problem, however. There was no bathroom. But the nice people who ran it let me go home regularly to relieve myself and return without paying. I saw *Maytime* with Jeanette McDonald and Nelson Eddy six times over two days. I suspect I was the theater's most devoted patron.

The theater lights eventually went dark. Too few people had money for entertainment. Our family found another cheap movie house. New Brighton adjoined Beaver Falls and the movie house there charged 25 cents a person for admission. The four of us could roll six miles down the road, coasting to keep the gas expenditure at almost nothing, get into the movies for a dollar and only have to burn gas to return home. Our favorite shows were movie versions of the operettas, usually with Jeanette McDonald starring. I also was fond of Sonja Henie, the ice skater. We saw all the Shirley Temple movies. For only a dollar, our family had an hour or two of magic.

The summer between fourth and fifth grade, the kids were carrying around Big-Little books. These books were four inches square and at least two inches thick. I don't remember what they cost but Mother vetoed them on account of the price. So I looked around the house for a book to read and carry around with me. Come to think of it, what a good fad for children to have.

Mother had a copy of *A Tale of Two Cities*. I appropriated it and began to read it. The first hundred pages were rough going. But as I toted it with me, I got a lot of comment. "Look what Flossie is reading. I didn't read that until I was twenty." So I kept reading. After the first part, I flew through the book and was hooked on Dickens. I read everything he had written and loved every bit. As I neared the end of a book, I would feel sad to be finishing and leaving all the characters.

When I entered school that Fall, I resented it because it interfered with my reading. I am still a little slow with mathematical calculations. I was too busy reading Dickens to bother memorizing all the tables when I was the proper age for it. As an adult I haven't been handicapped, however. I've had the good fortune to have two daughters who are math whizzes. They did the statistical calculations for my thesis and dissertation and now I own a calculator and a computer. And the characters in Dicken's stories remain in my memory as though they are people I knew long ago and fondly remember.

My parents bought me a violin and I began to take lessons. As much as I loved music, I was never very good at making it. I have a good ear and was always painfully aware that my pitch was often off. Daddy would listen to my music lessons and when the teacher left, he would pick up my half sized fiddle and play much better than I could.

I kept trying and played in the orchestra when I reached high school. I was the last of the second violins which meant I never got to play the melody. The violin is my favorite instrument and isn't it strange, I eventually married a man who plays the violin.

Chapter 9

Life as Viewed from the Apartment and The Move to the Brick House

Even though we were twenty-two steps above the street, and in the back of the building, it seemed as though we were in the middle of everything that happened in town.

The only tavern in Koppel was directly across from us. They had a new juke box which was played, *loud*, all day and all night. What music do I hear in my head as I remember those days? *Sweet Violets* drowns everything else out. Sweet Violets was a euphemism for s__t. It began, "Sweeter than all the roses...", described a number of embarrassing situations, and ended, "covered all over from head to foot, covered all over with sweet violets."

The first fifty times Johnny and I heard it, it tickled us. But the humor wore thin after a thousand hearings. All the rest of our lives if we wanted to communicate a s__ty thought to the other, we'd mention sweet violets.

On Saturday night or late Sunday morning, we would hear the sounds of drunken fights or rioting. We didn't have a window on the street so we didn't know exactly what was happening. We'd cover our heads with pillows and drift back to sleep. The next day someone would tell us what had occurred.

On summer nights, I liked to sleep on the porch. I especially liked to watch thunder storms from the day bed where I slept. There were other interesting sights as well.

Across the alley was the back of a house where a German bachelor lived. He was a plump middle aged man but he must have had some special attraction that a nine year old couldn't see. He'd get drunk on Saturday night and parade around nude in his back bedroom with the blind up. Most often he'd have company, one week a blond and another a brunette.

One hot summer night my parents sat up late on the porch and witnessed the show. After that, I was hustled off to the stuffy ward to sleep on Saturday nights.

Two doors down from the saloon, at the corner of the building, there was a bocci ball court. Bocci ball is an Italian bowling game played on a hard packed clay court. The Italian men collected there in the evening to play and to gossip. Even though I couldn't understand the words, I liked the sound of their musical voices, and the laughter and good humor of the game.

The Italian children in our class celebrated every birthday with a party. (We old Americans were deprived and only had family parties.) The whole class and the classes of the birthday person's siblings would be invited. Mother would help me buy some small gift and then I'd dress up in my yellow butterfly dress or the crisp organdy I wore when I outgrew my all-time favorite yellow taffeta. The menu was always the same, baloney sandwiches with mustard, red jello and cake. It tasted wonderful. Then we'd pin the tail on the donkey to the sound of happy shrieks and laughter. The final game was spin the bottle. The person who was *it* would spin the bottle, and when it stopped, the person toward whom it was pointed was kissed, and then became *it*. Then the birthday person would open his/her gifts and we'd go home, hoping someone else would have a birthday soon.

The Italian wakes were equally expressive but were sad rather than joyous. I remember houses jammed with rows of weeping women, sitting on straight chairs. The women were dressed in dull black cotton and they wore no jewelry or makeup. Their eyes were red and swollen and sobs were audible. I clung to my mother's hand as we passed by, pausing as she offered condolences. We'd enter the darkened room where the body lay in the casket, surrounded by candles. There would be more crying women. The men would be outside under the grape arbors, drinking wine and looking solemn.

We were in Koppel seven years which was long enough to see the transformation that marriage brought for many of the Italian women during that era. In their late teens they were beautiful. Their thick dark hair, flashing eyes and warm skin made them seem even more attractive than movie stars. I wanted to look like them when I grew up. Then there would be a big Italian wedding and a little later a pregnancy. Since there were large extended families, someone was sure to die. The colorful clothing would be discarded and the bride would begin wearing the dull black cotton dresses. The long hair would be pulled into a bun and the warm skin would turn sallow. The beautiful girl would be gone and in her place, a dull Italian matron.

Thank Heavens, customs have changed and this no longer happens.

The Christmas we lived in the apartment, I had ordered a Shirley Temple doll from my parents. We were all great admirers of that talented child. Mother shopped carefully at sales looking for Shirley Temple dresses for me. The only word that describes the intensity of my longing and anticipation for that doll is lust. I knew that my parents would get me the doll and I wanted it *now*. I couldn't wait for Christmas.

I searched the apartment and found nothing. Christmas was coming soon. Where had they hidden it? Maybe it was at the Perrillo's. Mother was great friends with Tassy, Theresa Perrillo. They had been a well off Italian family who owned grocery stores. There was only one store left and it wasn't doing well. Their parents had died and the four adult siblings lived in a beautiful large house. Eva was a teacher, later my seventh grade teacher, one brother ran the store, another worked for the state and Tassy kept house for the family. I loved their beautiful house, with its thick carpet and tasteful furniture. Later when I read about Italian aristocracy, the image of the Perrillos came to mind.

Two days before Christmas, overcome by my desire for my gift, I went to the Perrillos and knocked. I announced to Tassy that I had come for my Christmas present. She invited me into the kitchen. The floor and most of the walls were covered with white tile, the winter sun shone through the curtains and the room was thick with wonderful aromas. She invited me to sit down, found a large basket, lined it with waxed paper and preceded to fill it with the most wonderful cookies. There were pissettas, those crisp anis flavored waffle shaped cookies, deep fried wedding cookies, little pastry balls smothered in honey and wonderful stuffed cookies. She covered over the basket with a cloth and tied a red ribbon on the handle. There was no doll. Chastened and ashamed I carried our family's Christmas gift home from the Perrillo's.

When Mother came home I confessed and she promised to explain my bad manners to Tassy.

All of my adult life, I have made Italian cookies to celebrate Christmas.

The next night was Christmas Eve. I waited in the late afternoon darkness for Mother to come home. As soon as I heard her footsteps on the stairs, I rushed into the hall. Along with her purse and a bag of groceries, she carried the doll. Tired and worn out by my pleas, she handed it to me.

Shirley served me well as a favorite toy. When I had children I gave her to them, and they loved her until she was battered and worn. I do feel a slight twinge of regret when I see how much genuine Shirley Temple dolls sell for now. But only a twinge. She could never be worth more than she was to me when I played with her.

As Easter neared, the drug store next to the hardware store decorated the window. The centerpiece was an elegant rabbit, dressed in a vest and frock coat. I loved him. I pressed my nose against the window and longed for him. Daddy noticed my obsession and approached the druggist. He said he'd sell him to Dad for a dollar, but he'd have to wait until Easter, well maybe, the night before.

I dreamed about my bunny. I was actually afraid that I would die before Easter came. As an adult and a psychiatric nurse, I've wondered about my lust for the toy. Perhaps it was related to my loss of my little blue bunny or my love for my father. Mother couldn't understand how anyone could want anything that much.

But Daddy understood. Years later he told me that when he was a child, he had been given a new suit of clothes. His mother forbad him to wear them until Sunday mass. He said he couldn't sleep or even eat, so intense was his anticipation. His parents thought he was sick.

Easter Saturday we went to the drug store in the late afternoon. The rabbit was gone, sold to someone else. Dad put me in the car and rushed to the toy store in Beaver Falls. All they had left was two little bunnies. He got them for me. I was grateful that he understood and cared, but they were a poor substitute for my elegant bunny.

I don't think that I have since wanted any material object as much as I wanted that toy. Thank goodness!

Boyish bobs were in style. Mother looked at my long thick hair, which I found hard to keep combed and clean and told me how perky and cute I'd look with short curly hair. Maybe she was influenced by the fact that Aunt Thelma had spent half an hour scrubbing the grime off the back of my neck. Evidently I had neglected to lift up my shoulder length hair to wash it.

So I was convinced and one summer day walked up to the barbershop. I was wearing my usual summer costume, cut off denim coveralls that had been Johnny's. My feet were bare.

The barbershop was full of men who conversed with the barber, gossiped, argued politics and had a generally good time. I got in the chair and told the barber I wanted a boyish bob. He began clipping away and talking.

When he was finished I looked in the mirror. I was horrified. I didn't have a boyish bob, I had a short boy cut. I paid him and left. As I walked down the street I met a neighborhood teenaged boy who looked at me and said, "Hi John, How ya doin'?"

If I told Johnny he'd kill me. If I told my parents, they would laugh about it and Johnny would hear. So I kept my humiliation, tightly locked inside me, until my hair grew out and Johnny had grown much taller than I.

Mother and Dad were invited to a formal party. Dad obtained a tuxedo somewhere. Knowing Dad, he probably bought it on credit and returned it after the party. Mother borrowed a pink satin dress from Eva Perrillo. It was heavy satin, cut on the bias and skin tight.

Mother tried it on. She looked beautiful, just like a movie star. But her girdle showed. She tried it with panties—same problem. The halter top allowed no space for a bra. Fortunately Mother was well endowed above the waist and sagged very little. Then she slipped on the dress over her nude body. She looked gorgeous. But what was that bump just below her abdomen? Off she went to the bathroom with a pair of scissors. A few snips and she really looked like a movie star.

Daddy, who looked very elegant, went down the stairs to the street to move the car as close to the door as possible. The men in the bar saw him and came outside to see why Joe Fisher was dressed in a monkey suit. Dad went back up to escort Mother to the car. Johnny and I, dressed in our usual denim coveralls followed them down the stairs. By then the drug store patrons and the hardware man had joined the crowd. There were gasps and then applause as Mother came out the door. Dad opened the car door for her and helped her in. Fortunately bias cuts cling to one's body but they do give under pressure so Mother was able to sit. Dad carefully closed the door, went to the driver's side, offered a slight wave to the audience, got in and drove away.

The people drifted back inside, hoping that some other interesting thing would happen that evening. Johnny and I went back upstairs. I think I floated up; I was so proud of my parents.

Johnny and I were not required to do chores. But we were expected to be able to take care of ourselves. We could make simple meals and clean up to the extent that we put the milk in the refrigerator and the dishes in the sink. Mother and Dad did the wash, rolling the washing machine from the ward, through the hall and into the kitchen. In summer the washing was hung on the porch. In winter it hung in the ward. Ironing was done by whoever wanted a garment to wear. Dad did his shirts, and if there were a special occasion that I needed a dress for, he ironed it for me. Otherwise we pressed what we needed when we needed it.

I envied the kids whose mothers stayed at home, cooked for them and ironed their clothes. Yet I was proud of my mother and grateful that she supported the family and kept us together.

After we had lived in the apartment several years we moved to a house. It was one of the nicest houses in town. A bootlegger had owned it and when he was arrested, the Federal Government took it and rented it out. A rather snooty family had lived there before us.

The house was buff brick and sat directly across from the school. Its general plan was similar to the yellow house, but it finished more beautifully. There was a large sun porch, hard wood floors, French doors and tiled bath and kitchen. And best of all, I was to have my own room.

The first night we slept in the brick house, however, I had to sleep with my mother. We unpacked and spread the sheets on the bed and crawled in exhausted. Just as I drifted off to sleep, I jumped as a stinging pain pierced my arm. Mother stirred and I announced that something had bitten me. She mumbled, "Go to sleep."

But I couldn't! I squirmed and scratched. Mother became increasingly annoyed. She wasn't being bitten. It must be my imagination.

After a while, she wearily told me to get up and turn on the light. I did and discovered I was ablaze with red raised welts.

Mother tore back the covers and saw little red beetles run for cover. She captured one. Bed bugs!

We didn't sleep much. The next day Dad went to the federal office and told them the story. They gave him a powder to sprinkle around the baseboards. Evidently the hungry little pests lived in the walls but could not pass the powder barrier without becoming fatally ill.

It worked. That was the last of the bed bugs. When we met the people who had lived there before, we wondered, about them. How had they withstood those hungry little varmints?

My parents bought me a Jenny Lind bed and an antique wash stand. Daddy picked out a print of a little girl in a yellow dress, a copy of Reynolds painting, *The Age of Innocence*, and hung it over my bed. I had a bookcase for my favorite books and room for all my treasures. I loved my room.

One night I lit a candle and knelt down to pray, just like my friend, Mrs. DeSanzo. Wouldn't you know it, that was the night that my brother decided to see what I did when I was alone in my room and peeked through the key hole. Then he teased me and threatened to tell my friends. This time, I offered counter threats and said I'd just make up whoppers and tell all his friends. Neither of us carried out the threats.

Siblings do help one learn to cope.

Chapter 10

Johnny's Travails, Moving to Grandma John's and Starting a New School

Dad and I had developed a new game, although at the time I didn't realize it was a game. One of us would remark about some item of news, from the radio or the newspaper, and express an opinion. The other would take the opposite view and we would be off into a heated debate. It was a no-holds-barred match with personal insults acceptable. It didn't take me long to learn that when Dad got personal, I was winning. Mother and Johnny would stay out of the fray, but they found the whole thing amusing.

The next day we two debaters might go at the subject again, but this time we would take the opposite side and I would find myself arguing against the point of view and rationale I had expressed the day before. Johnny told me that when we did this we looked identical, even though I more strongly resemble my mother.

Daddy died more than forty years ago and I've never found anyone with whom I could have a good argument, one like I had with my father. The training served me well. I don't get upset in the presence of verbal aggression and if anything, can think more clearly and present a more logical case. I have also learned however, that most people avoid verbal combat, and don't see my debating skill as an endearing trait. Had I become a lawyer, rather than a nurse, I might have been better able to use the skills this family game taught me.

John's arguments with Dad were real, not stylized debates and frequently ended in punishment. The punishment was seldom physical because Johnny had found a way to defuse it. He would look at Dad and quote a line from the radio show, *Fibber McGee and Molly*. It was, "You're a hard man, McGee." Invariably when Dad heard that he would be amused and the punishment would be scaled down to a loss of privilege. Some people thought that my dad's name was McGee Fisher.

Johnny acquired a washing machine motor, a small gasoline motor. He was fascinated by it and proceeded to build himself a little car. It was rather crudely made, a plank for a body and wheels from someone's wagon, but it ran. He drove it all around town, followed by a crowd of boys who begged to be allowed to drive it. He would pull up to a gas station and say, "Fill 'er up", pay the man a nickel for the fuel and then drive off. This went on for a week, until the police told him he needed a driver's license to operate a motor vehicle on the town's streets.

He removed the motor from the cart and began to overhaul it. He tried all sorts of fuel mixtures in it. This occurred in the summer and putt, putt, putt and bang, bang, bang echoed through the neighborhood. The neighbors complained about the noise. Mother was afraid that John would blow himself up or burn down the garage. Dad was tired of the whole affair.

Dad took the motor, drove up along the highway and threw it into a wooded ravine.

My heart ached for Johnny. Motors were the only thing that John was good at. He was failing in school and his little sister not only was in the same class, but led it. One day he was the town hero, the kid everyone wanted to be near. The next day, he was the kid who was picked last when someone chose sides for a team.

I wondered how it was that my father, who was so sensitive to my needs and understanding of my irrational yearnings, could be so blind to his son's.

After a while, without my parents knowledge, John turned his attention to electrical experiments.

One day, Dad went outside to look at something in the front yard. He turned back to the house and reached for the door to the sun porch. He looked surprised, hesitated and reached again—and was zapped with a jolt of electricity. Johnny had rigged up that little surprise.

This little joke was supposed to be all in fun. As an adult, John told me that it was more. It was a warning to Dad, to back off and show more respect for John's needs and wants.

John must have been thirteen then. This incident has a familiar feel. When my husband was seventeen he had an argument with his father. Verl had saved money to go to college and he also wanted to spend some of his savings to buy a car. His dad said, "No car." They argued. Verl hit his father. His dad, a powerful man, reciprocated and sent him sprawling. Verl bought the car and went off to college, paying his own way for four years. Is this the way males declare their independence from their fathers?

Incidentally, Verl's father bought him a car for a graduation gift.

The worst of the depression was past. Mother was still working and Dad actually sold an insurance policy or two. He was home less and spent a lot of time driving around.

One night some men came to the door and asked for Dad. He wasn't there. They sat in a car in the driveway and waited for him. Mother was very worried. Finally Dad came home and talked with the men outside. Then he came in the house and told Mother he needed a hundred dollars. For some reason, Mother had a few of Aunt Florey's checks. She went upstairs and carefully copied Aunt Florey's signature on it and gave it to Dad. The men left.

I will never be certain what was going on, but I suspect that Dad and the men had been kiting checks. Before the days of electronic transmission between banks, it took longer for checks to clear. It was possible to cash a check at one bank, draw on another and not have any money in the account. If a group of people did it, it was possible to keep cash flowing for a while. But the day would come when there would have to be money to cover the checks.

I knew how honest my mother was. She had been raised by John Baird, the straightest man in the county. It must have been terribly difficult for her to steal from her adopted mother. How could Daddy have gotten himself in such a mess, that she was forced to do that to protect him? I was disappointed yet sadly accepting of the things my father did.

My parents were troubled every Sunday evening when they returned from our weekly excursion to Aunt Florey's. She was in her late seventies and while she had always been strange, she seemed more forgetful and confused. It was impossible to know if the changes in her were due to her psychological isolation or if they were physical. She had been alone for several years since Uncle John's death. She didn't read books and she had no radio. All day long she sat in the large rocking chair and talked to herself. The minister called occasionally and if she were ill, Dr. Mitchell would make a house call. John spent the summer with her but for nine months of the year, she was alone.

Mrs. Latshaw lived next door. Mother persuaded Aunt Florey to hire her to clean and shop for her groceries. Mother wondered if Aunt Florey's check covered the cost of the Latshaw's groceries as well. But that was the price that had to be paid in this situation.

Bill Hedegar, the man who managed the oil and gas wells began to drop around to see her occasionally. Bill, who was in his late forties, had never married. Then one Sunday, Aunt Florey said that Bill had mentioned how nice it would be if they were married and he were living there.

Suddenly Mother had visions of losing her inheritance. She had been given to Uncle John and Aunt Florey when she was four because they wanted an heir. Although her own mother and father stayed in touch, legally she was her uncle's child. She had endured going to elementary school in tattered clothes and dirty hair, because Aunt Florey didn't know enough or care enough to see that she was clean. She had been separated from her sister and brothers and raised as an only child on an isolated farm. Uncle John was a fine man and a good father. Aunt Florey was more like his child than a marital partner. She had been affectionate with Mother when she was a small girl, but as Mother grew, Aunt Florey was jealous of Uncle John's love for his adopted daughter. After enduring all that, was she going to lose the money, the farm and the security?

The decision was made that we would move to the country, live with Aunt Florey and take care of her.

I was in seventh grade. I led my class and liked the school. There was no high school in Koppel and in another year, I would be attending school in Elwood City or Beaver Falls. I enjoyed my friends, but I did not have a very special best friend. So the thought of leaving the town did not upset me. What did cause me grief was leaving the nice house and my very own room.

Aunt Florey's house was a pleasant brick California bungalow. The furniture in it was the furniture that had been bought in the 1880's. There was no couch in the living room, just a group of rocking chairs, a secretary with books that hadn't been read for fifty years, a library table and a piano. Aunt Florey was fond of house plants and they were massed in front of every window.

There was a formal dining room with dining room furniture and a day bed, where my father slept. The kitchen was small and crowded, too small for the family to eat an evening meal. A back sun porch served as a dinette during the warm months. There were three bedrooms, Aunt Florey's, John's and the guest room, which I shared with my mother.

I loved my mother but at twelve, I didn't want to share a room with her. Even worse, I didn't want to sleep with her. And she wasn't any happier about the arrangement than I was.

The room was crowded with old fashioned oak furniture and a huge, table-high, eight foot long cedar chest. The only space was the aisle between the bed and the chest and dresser. The closet was tiny.

The house had a bathroom and running water. The gas fixtures had been replaced by electricity. Both the stove and refrigerator were powered by natural gas from our own wells.

Mother and Dad had sold most of their furniture and stored the things they wanted to keep. They returned a partially paid for refrigerator to the store, an act that caused them to be haunted with a bad credit rating for the rest of their lives. Aunt Florey wanted nothing changed, so we had very little to remind us of our home.

We did bring the radio and slipped it quietly into the dining room.

We moved the first of April 1938, when I was in seventh grade. The first night I stayed with Grandma Tom and caught the bus in front of her house. But after that, I was introduced to the Van Tassel girls who lived on an adjoining farm and we walked more than a mile to catch the school bus. I say walked, but speed walked would be more accurate. I was accustomed to running out the front door, across the street and into the school. My new companions seemed to take pride in making the trip to and from the school bus in the least time possible. I was exhausted by the time I reached the school.

The six week term was almost over when I arrived and I had missed most of it. Although the classes had the same names as the classes in Koppel, the units they had been studying were different. At the end of the period, I received the first and last D's I have ever been given.

The other students, of course, all knew each other. Although they were spread all over a large township, many went to the same church, Westfield Presbyterian. The Bairds had settled at the edge of the township and went to a Methodist Church in Hillsville. Although my mother's family had been there since the late 1700's, to my class mates I was that new strange Fisher girl.

Bob McFate was friendly, however. His aunt had been my mother's best childhood friend and college roommate. A generation before his grandfather and my grandfather had been best friends and neighbors. That is, until Old Bob McFate's dog killed forty of grandpa's prize sheep. That was what Grandpa John believed. He put poison in the carcasses and the dog came along, ate it and died. The two fast friends never spoke again. They did keep the fences between then strong and had no objection to their families being friendly. Whenever the opportunity arose, they inquired about the other.

Young Bob was a rosy cheeked blue-eyed boy with curly blonde hair. He welcomed me to the class and I began to feel more comfortable.

Sports were big at Mt Jackson and every recess someone would break out a ball and bat. If it were cold, we would shoot baskets. Gym class was the same. I had never played sports and was completely inept. In fact if a ball came my way, particularly a hard thrown one, I didn't try to catch it; I ducked. When we played softball, I was the extra person in the outfield and I prayed that no ball would come my way.

I was a good swimmer and a skilled roller skater of the sidewalk variety. I rode my bike several miles to visit my Grandma and Grandpa Tom. There was no pool at Mt. Jackson and no sidewalks. So besides being an outsider in the school and making my first Ds, I was the last person chosen for any teams.

However, at the end of the next six week period I made all As and led the class.

I had problems with spelling. I still do. Everyday we had a dozen or so new spelling words. I scribbled them on a tablet among a lot of other scribbles and left them out on the desk during the daily quiz. It was the first time I had ever cheated. Miss Fullerton came by my desk as she called out the words and noticed my tablet. After the quiz, she announced that from now on all books and materials must be cleared from the desk before the quizzes. I was deeply shamed and profoundly grateful that she hadn't embarrassed me in front of the class. I never cheated again.

Several years later she was teaching my Freshman English class. We were studying Ivanhoe. She mixed up the plot. I had already read it and was familiar with the story. I didn't want to embarrass her and I was afraid if she continued another student would realize her mistake and tell her. So after class I approached her and told her that I was confused about the plot. I explained my impression and asked her to help straighten me out. She looked back through the book and realized her mistake. She thanked me warmly. Miss Fullerton may not have been the world's best literature teacher but she was a role model for graciousness.

A few days before our first Easter at Mt. Jackson, our family went to town, New Castle, to shop. Dad and I were together in the 5 and 10 store. Plush bunnies were displayed at the toy counter. They weren't elegant like the the bunny I had lusted after a few years before and they were female bunnies dressed in print dresses. But I liked them, as a decoration rather than a toy. Daddy responded by buying one, for one dollar.

Mother met us there a few minutes after the transaction. She was angry. "Flossie, you are too old for something like that."

I moved into my protective shell, but her words did hurt.

Then one of my teachers happened by. I don't know where Mother had met her, but they chatted a while. Mother told her about the bunny and she agreed that I was too old for a stuffed animal. Dad wandered off to look at the tools. Even the shell that Aunt Florey had helped me develop didn't protect me from humiliation.

The Perillos invited me to come back to Koppel for a visit when school was over. Eva had been my seventh grade teacher. She was a very bright stylish woman. Her long black hair was parted in the middle, and pulled back into a bun. She wore stylish clothes on her tall slim figure. I thought she looked like the Italian countesses I read about in my books. Tassy was a warm comfortable person. I was delighted at their invitation.

The first morning after I arrived, I got up from the day bed in Eva's large upstairs bedroom where I slept, put on my robe and headed toward the bathroom. Just as I got to the door, it clicked shut. One of the brothers had gone in. I went back to the bedroom and waited, growing increasingly desperate to urinate. The bathroom occupant sang, showered, shaved and probably primped. An hour passed. By then I was in agony.

I felt my sphincter weaken and moved off the oriental rug to the hard wood floor. The dam burst and I flooded the floor.

Desperate to hide my sin, I searched the closet and found a box of kotex. I sopped up the urine with three or four pads. By now the bathroom was empty.

I put one pad down the toilet and then thought better of it and put the others in the bottom of the waste basket.

It wasn't long before someone discovered that the toilet was clogged up. I couldn't bring myself to tell anyone what happened. Eventually a plumber was called and the pad was found. Tassy found the others. Everyone was furious at me, not so much because I had stopped up the toilet and cost them money and time, but because I refused to confess.

I just couldn't. I was contrite and so terribly sorry I had done what I had done. Couldn't they see that? Why was it necessary for me to abase myself further and tell them I had wet myself? I knew that I was the worst possible house guest and that I'd never be invited back. I knew that people I liked and admired would now dislike me. But the words wouldn't come.

Tassy was cool to me the rest of the week and Eva was away most of the time. I was glad when the week was over and Dad came back for me. I was never invited back.

Chapter 11

Life in the Country, Aunt Florey Dies

About a year after we moved to Aunt Florey's, we learned that the Hoffmasters were moving back to their farm.

The Hoffmaster's ancestor, a young man named Wright had acquired the farm before the Revolutionary War. He had traded a horse, saddle and bridle for 350 acres of Western Pennsylvania land. When he wrote his mother about his new possession, she wrote back and chided him for wasting good Virginia horse flesh on a worthless piece of forest.

The farm prospered. The log house was replaced by a 21 room brick house with marble fireplaces and beautiful walnut and chestnut wood work and paneling. There was an ice house, so that the Wrights could have ice cream all summer and a greenhouse to supply flowers and vegetables during the winter. The Wrights were the community's gentry.

The Bairds, mother's family, arrived right after the Revolution. As the generations passed, their holdings were split up among the children. Grandpa Tom and Grandpa John were born in the original log house. The Bairds were a respected family, but not gentry like the Wrights. Lizzy Wright married Albert Hoffmaster, a cousin of Aunt Florey's. They had no children so they adopted Wright, who was a few years younger than Mother. Wright did not learn that he was adopted until he was a teenager and a drunken man informed him. His natural parents and siblings were alive and he had met the man he later learned was his father. This was profoundly upsetting to him, just as mother's unusual family situation had been to her.

Wright's mother viewed farming as an occupation beneath her class. She sent Wright to college, hoping he would be a minister. The farm and beautiful house were rented and neglected. Now Lizzie was dead, and Wright, his wife Mae, and two children were moving back to the farm to fulfill Wright's dream of returning to the land.

Mae had been one of Mother's college roommates and they had also roomed together when they were young teachers. Mae's daughter Eleanor was a year younger than I and her little brother, Albert, was about nine. We greeted their return with happy anticipation.

Eleanor was a tall girl, with clear blue eyes, lovely skin and light brown hair. Even as a child she was practical, down to earth, and unflappable. We became and still are good friends.

Her father was a kind, gentle man, who was patient with his children. Eleanor and Albert settled into farm living immediately and happily.

Mae, Eleanor's mother, had a Puritanical streak and a controlling nature. I sometimes felt sorry for Wright and their children. Yet I always liked Mae and felt welcome in their home. I listened to her lectures about what I should do, knowing that I would be on my way home shortly and out of Mae's control. I interpreted her bossiness as interest in my welfare. I was glad, however, that she wasn't my mother.

We bought our milk from Hoffmasters. Every other evening I walked half a mile to their place, carrying my empty gallon jug. It would be filled and set in the cooler because I was never ready to go directly home. Often it would be dark when I left. There were no houses along the route and there were few cars. If I saw the lights of a car approach, I would step across the ditch and hide in the bushes or behind a tree.

Shortly after the Hoffmasters arrived, Wright bought a pony, Duchess. Duchess was four years old and had never been ridden. Wright did train her enough so that he, Eleanor and a few strong neighborhood boys could stay on her back—most of the time. My attempts were quickly brushed off, literally. Duchess would head for a tree with a low limb and get rid of that offending 100 pounds on her back. But trying to ride her and watching other people try did provide excitement.

The farm teemed with babies, little chickens and ducks, kittens, calves who sucked your fingers and noisily slurped down their milk and pink baby pigs. One little pig had been lain on by its careless mother and had to be nursed back to health in the house. Eleanor and I fed it with a bottle and it became a pet, a house broken one, until it was too big for the kitchen and went back to the barn.

Eleanor had more chores than I had, and when I visited, I helped her. I helped with the canning and learned to render lard, so that my friend could be free to play.

Since Eleanor and I were in different classes at school, we developed different sets of friends. But after school, on the weekends and in the summer, Eleanor was my favorite companion. Sixty years later, we are still friends.

Bob Mc Fate liked Eleanor a great deal. When they were old enough they dated each other. In the summer, Bob would ride one of his family's big work horses the mile from his family's farm to visit Eleanor. Since I was often there, the three of us would pile on the horse's broad back and ride through the fields and woods. At least these gentle giants didn't try to brush me off. Although once I stood too close and the huge fellow accidentally stepped on my foot. Ouch!

In the winter, if there were a heavy snow fall, Bob would arrive in a sleigh. We would ride all through the snow clogged roads. I often drove the horse, enabling Bob and Eleanor to neck.

The atmosphere at home was gloomy. Mother was depressed and Aunt Florey was increasingly difficult.

Hoffmasters was a happy place and a welcome respite.

Aunt Florey didn't want us there. Yet there seemed to be no other solution. One time Mother was washing the kitchen walls. It was a hot hard job so she opened the window. Aunt Florey came into the room, and said, "That window had never been opened," and hit Mother, hard.

Another time we went to a church picnic. We had started attending the church in Hillsville where Aunt Florey and Uncle John had once gone. Aunt Florey said she was too sickly to go with us. When we came home at eight in the evening, she had locked the doors and wouldn't let us in. Dad managed to open the cellar door and we went inside. The happy time we'd had at the picnic was quickly forgotten.

When we were in Koppel, I often felt sorry for my mother because she worked so hard. Now that she wasn't working, I became aware that she really liked her work and was happier doing it.

Dad was still selling insurance and doing better at it. However, in our room at night, Mother still wrote checks and carefully copied Aunt Florey's name. What they paid for were things for Johnny and me. She bought us bicycles. Sometime later, I heard Aunt Florey talking to herself about the nice bikes she had gotten us. I never knew if she had found the canceled check and assumed she had written and forgotten writing them, or if there were some other solution.

I hated sleeping with Mother and I know that sleeping with me was unpleasant for her.

One night I dreamed that I needed desperately to urinate. In my dream I ran and ran to reach an outhouse. Once inside I plopped down on the seat and with great relief began to void.

Mom's scream woke me up and I leaped over her and ran down the hall to the bathroom. When I came back, she was changing the bed. The expression, "mad as a wet hen" perfectly describes the way she looked.

When I was a high school freshman, I got chicken pox. I had dried itchy lesions all over my body. At night they itched and I scratched and wiggled.

"Flossie, for heaven's sake, stop scratching. You are driving me wild."

I couldn't stop. So after a while, I got up, felt my way down the dark hall to the living room. We had a gas stove in the fireplace. I lit it and sat in the dark the rest of the night, scratching.

I had a cat, a black tom named Timmy. He liked to sleep with me, but Mother forbad it. Sometimes when I went to bed early, I would let him lie beside me, under the covers. One time, I went to sleep before I had put him outside through the window. Mother came in, saw a black furry head on the pillow beside mine, whipped off the covers and sent yowling Timmy racing down the hall.

When I had been a little girl, I loved to sleep with either parent. But a teenaged girl who is trying to establish her own identity and a harried, worried mother need more space between them than a shared bed allows.

Dad's nightmares were something I took for granted when I was younger. Now that I was a teenager, I understood how dangerous and upsetting they were. Dad would begin screaming in the middle of the night. Then I would hear Mother calling, "Flossie, Johnny, get the light." One or both of us would dash to the room where Dad had been sleeping and turn on the light. Mother would be holding on to Dad, trying to prevent him from hurting himself.

Usually Dad screamed, "Oh My God, it's coming down!." Sometimes it was "Jesus Christ, don't throw that!" The most upsetting of all was, "I'll save you, Dear!"

When the last was said, it meant that one of us was in Daddy's arms and he was headed for the door or window. He never hurt us, but he did hurt himself. Once he ran down the hall to the living room and into the brick fireplace. He knocked himself out.

Usually, he would awaken, look around with a confused expression for an instant and then say, "I guess I had a nightmare."

Then we would all return to our beds, wondering about the awful things that had happened to Daddy to leave such scars on his mind.

There were happy times, in spite of the nightmares, Mom's gloom and the difficulty of living with Aunt Florey. Uncle John had planted fruit trees on the acre lot, and no one enjoyed them more than I did. Some of my fondest memories are of waking up on a summer morning, dressing hurriedly, and going outside for breakfast. Depending on the season, I might have succulent peaches, Royal Ann cherries, apples, grapes or plums. Dad planted a large garden

Florence Hardesty

and we also had strawberries. The rhubarb patch contributed stewed rhubarb, rhubarb juice which was pink and tasted like lemonaid, and the fruit for wonderful pies and cobblers.

Mother canned the fruit and the tomatoes from the garden. Dad gave the extra plums to an Italian man who lived in Hillsville and was given a bottle of plum wine in return.

I wasn't expected to help with any of the daily family chores. Mother did all the inside work and Dad did the outside. I kept my room clean and kept out of the way.

One beautiful summer day, I was sitting on the first branch of the big maple tree in the front yard. I was obscured by the leaves and an open book was perched on my knee. Mother came to the front door and called, "Flossie!" I didn't answer. Then she muttered to herself, "I never know where that kid is." Settled in my leafy bower, I turned my attention to the book.

Doing the wash was such a huge task that I was expected to help. The well that supplied the water for the house had a problem. It was contaminated with oil. The limestone quarries were still a mile away, but they did heavy blasting, drilling holes in the stone and then setting charges of dynamite. The sound of the blasts was a normal part of life, as was the fine limestone dust that covered the trees and shrubs. Evidently the explosions had cracked the strata of the rock and allowed oil from our wells to seep into the aquifer. We drank the water, and cooked with it, ignoring the iridescent sheen the oil made as it floated on the surface of the water. But we couldn't get clothes clean in the oily water.

We had a cistern that collected the water from the slate roof and ran into an in-ground holding tank. This water was soft, but not safe to drink.

On wash day, we pumped water from the cistern into buckets, carried them down the stairs into the basement, and poured them into a high boiler that sat atop a gas hot plate. When the water was hot, it was dipped out by the bucketful and poured into the washer and rinse tubs. Then Mother ran the washer and ran the clothes through the spinner, before they were rinsed and spun again. I was the one who carried them up the steps to the outside and hung them on the clothes lines to dry.

Mother had heavy menstrual periods, and besides that, kotex were expensive, so she had flannel cloths she used during her monthly period. Even though she soaked them in a bucket of cold water in the bathroom, they were still stained. The lines would be full with more precious clothing so Mom's rags would be distributed around the yard, on bushes or in the tall grass of the field next door, to dry and be bleached by the sun. I was always afraid that someone important, like a boy, would happen into our back yard and see our washing.

Ironing continued to remain a do-it-yourself job.

In North Beaver Township School, girls were required to take two years of Home Economics. I thought it was a little strange that my mother was qualified to teach Home Economics, and yet I had to spend so much of the school day learning things she could teach me. I did want to maintain my position at the top of the class so I learned to make white sauce, baking powder biscuits, etc. I also learned how one makes pies but I must confess, I was a D - pie maker. I hated Bertha Vinkler, who made pies at home and was an expert. She made these beautiful creations and walked around the room, balancing them on one hand. I had fantasies about tripping her.

My mother was an expert seamstress. She was so fussy and meticulous that I gave up trying to learn from her. However my Home Ec. teacher wasn't so demanding and I did make a blouse and an apron. I discovered that it wasn't so hard.

At school I made friends with a small, shy girl named Evelyn Strohecker. Her mother had burned to death, in Evelyn's presence when she was two. I suspect that Evelyn didn't have any particular friend before I arrived.

When we moved from eighth grade to high school, I began to notice that boys were attractive. I wanted to enlarge my friendship group and to spend time with girls who would attract boys and help me to learn how to behave in a mixed group. I talked about this with Evelyn and we discussed which clique we would attempt to join. We decided to become better friends with Virginia Lee Stump.

Virginia Lee was a tall, blonde girl who was a talented pianist. She also was very popular. Evelyn and

I moved into her circle. At first, I made sure to include Evelyn, but later, as Ginny and I became better friends, she was often not included. I don't think Evelyn ever forgave me for deserting her. She was never at our class reunions but I obtained her address and wrote to her. She didn't answer.

I began to be aware of times when my parents were awash in a soft happy aura. One time I came home from school and went into the bed room. They were on the bed, smiling and relaxed. They said they had just taken a nap. I felt terribly uncomfortable, as though I had seen something I shouldn't have seen. In a few years, when I was more at home with my own sexuality, it pleased me to know that people as old as my parents still liked each other that way.

The Penwells were another family that I saw often. There were a lot of them. In all, Mr. and Mrs. Caldwell produced thirteen sons and two daughters.

Mrs. Penwell began her life as a procreator when she was fourteen. She was unmarried when her first child was born. She said it was Frank Penwell's but he wasn't sure. So he sent his mother to look at the baby. His mother returned home and said, "That child is a Penwell. Now you marry that girl!" He did. Their last son was born shortly after we came back to the farm.

This was the second such incident that had occurred in this small community. People often talk about the joys of a close knit rural community. There are many positives. But one of the negatives is that people never forget. One's transgressions might be remembered and talked about for generations.

At first the Penwells lived in a house my birth grandparents owned. There had been a barn and outbuildings when they moved there, but by the time they left, the barn and sheds were gone, and so was the porch railing and any other convenient piece of wood that could be used to supply heat.

Then they moved next door. The oldest boy bought a house for the parents. They took care of this house—the boys were older and it was a house they had put their money into. They were originally from southern Ohio, right across the border from Kentucky and they loved to hunt coon. You can't hunt coon without dogs, so we had seven coon hounds for neighbors. They were always penned but they sure could howl. At least seven cars were parked around the place. Old Frank Penwell, the father, was known to drink, but he always went to work in the morning. When his car wasn't running, he walked, a tall spare figure, moving swiftly down the road to the limestone quarries in Hillsville.

Every morning and late afternoon, I walked to and from the school bus accompanied by the Penwell boys and Cecely, their nine year old sister. The Van Tassels had moved and the pace was now more leisurely. Eleanor and Albert joined us when we passed their house. We laughed and joked as we trudged along. When I was thirteen, my first kiss—dry and quick—was delivered by Dale Penwell, a shy blonde boy, in Hoffmaster's barn while they were putting up hay. I never dated Dale, but I knew he admired me and I enjoyed it.

I had a special friend at school, Jim Hamilton. Jim was a quiet farm boy from the other end of the township. One of his hands was mutilated from a farm accident. In spite of that, he was skilled at drawing. In class, when the class was dull, Jim and I would doodle together. He would sketch something—often the teacher, and show it to me. Then I'd do my version of the same subject. On we would go, filling page after page with pictures.

I didn't think of Jim as a boyfriend. He was nice looking and I certainly liked him. Mother had told me about the boy who sat behind her when she was in high school, Jimmy Crawford. He had been very fond of her but she loved another. Time passed and she became an adult. The boy she had pined for had become a disreputable heavy drinking fellow and Jimmy was an eminent physician, the man who delivered my oldest child. I knew the story but it never occurred to me to take a hard look at James Hamilton. He became a well respected art teacher and school principal. Now I wonder, why it never occurred to me to view Jim as a boyfriend.

I became interested in boys in the eighth grade, but my body didn't cooperate. My hormones were sluggish. I had no breasts and I had not yet entered the sorority of monthly pads and I thought I never would become a woman. Mother assured me that it would happen; she'd been sixteen and Aunt Thelma even later.

I had a very small waist and rounded hips. I didn't consider this a liability until Johnny called attention to the fact that my small waist and big hips made me look abnormal, "sort of like an ant." I bristled at first but later I noticed that his eyes were sparkling with what looked like admiration.

Besides being a young woman in a child's body, I had another problem. My nose developed a hump, like my father's nose. I thought my chin was weak and with my huge nose, I didn't want anyone to see me in profile. I solved the problem by wearing my heavy wavy hair long and loose, almost like a veil.

Mother tried to console me by telling me that noses could be made straighter. Johnny said, "Yeah, Mom, but don't you think we should wait until she quits bumpin'?"

I was aware of but didn't agonize over my physical defects, my inexperience with boys or the fact that I wasn't the most popular girl in the class. A part of me observed this awkward teenager, and knew that she was essentially a good person and that she was smart. That part of me could almost chuckle with my parents about my teenaged foolishness. I knew that I would grow up and be fine.

Johnny spent some time with the Penwells but mostly he was off on his bike, to Bessmer, Hillsville, Edinburg or Mt. Jackson—the little towns that surrounded our place. He had friends in all four towns. Later, when he was in the Army all these towns listed him among their servicemen. As usual he wasn't doing well in school. But he was fixing the neighbors' cars for them and occasionally a farmer would consult him about a tractor or farm machine.

John had an old wreck of a car that someone had given him. It was a coupe with a rumble seat. John was too young to have a drivers license and the car wasn't licensed. But he would lower a can into one of the oil tanks on the farm, pull up some crude oil and use it for gasoline. We would drive around our farm which was across the road from the house or go half a mile or so on the road, the exhaust smoking and the motor protesting.

One day Dad was driving down the road and happened to come upon John riding his bike. Smoke trailed out behind and when he came abreast, Dad saw that John was smoking a pipe. Dad was amused. John never smoked in the house, and no one disapproved. Johnny was growing up.

John liked a girl in Edinburg. She was a few years older than he and from a family that married young and had lots of babies, sometimes in the reverse order. Mother and Dad were worried. There were rumors that our family had money—oil wells and a limestone lease. What if John got trapped in a situation and had to marry this girl.

The government had begun a program called the Civilian Conservation Corps. Young unemployed men were recruited, lived in Army barracks, were trained in skills, and performed useful work. They built trails in national forests, maintained camp grounds, and fought forest fires.

My parents introduced the idea to John and he thought he'd like to try it. So at sixteen, John joined the CCC. He was sent to Sligo, Pennsylvania. They had vocational teachers there and John took and excelled in every course. He learned basic machinist skills, carpentry, welding, and electrical skills. And he was the star of the class in mechanics.

Later he was sent to Priest Lake in Northern Idaho. He did some forestry there but mostly he took care of the logging equipment. In his spare time, he became acquainted with the owner of a speed boat, who let him tune the motor and race it.

I missed Johnny and worried that he must be lonesome, so far away from home and my parents. When we've talked as adults, he told me that he felt that our parents wanted to be rid of him. I think that they were worried about him and thought that this was the best solution available.

When I was a high school freshman, Aunt Florey died. She complained of a pain in her chest and Dr. Mitchell came to see her. He diagnosed her problem as a mild heart attack and recommended rest. The next evening our family was in the living room, listening to the radio, when we heard a noise. We rushed back to Aunt Florey's bedroom and found her half off the bed, dead. Evidently she had been getting up and had a second heart attack.

A few days later, her funeral was held and she was buried beside Uncle John. We returned home, and unable to wait even a decent interval, began to make changes. Dad went out to the front yard and with a sledge hammer broke the sewer pipe that had served as a planter. He'd always hated it. Our pictures, books and china came out of storage. Off we went to Sears Roebuck. We bought a living room couch, coffee table, rugs and lamps. And best of all, the oak bedroom set was given away and the cedar chest was carried to the cellar. A new maple bedroom set was installed in what had been Mother's and my room and once again, I had the luxury of my very own room.

I wrote a letter to Aunt Thelma, telling her about all our new acquisitions. She was shocked at my glee. Now that I am an adult and an old woman, I can see the situation from Aunt Florey's point of view. Then our pleasure was not because she was dead, but because all the difficulties of living there with a strange, senile old woman were over.

In some sense, although the depression lasted until we entered World War II, the depression was over for our family.

Chapter 12

Growing Up With Cousins, High School

During my early teens, I spent part of each summer visiting my Aunt Thelma and her family in Western New York. Mother arranged for these long summer visits, thinking that I needed to get away from the country and be with other young people. Then too my Aunt had no daughters and she welcomed my company.

Aunt Thelma lived in Hornell when I made my first visit and later moved to a farm near Arkport. Uncle Jack was working in the grocery store where he had begun his career. Cousin Billy was a year older than John and Jackie was a few years older.

Aunt Thelma struggled with health problems, but in spite of that she had a sunny disposition. Her house was always beautifully decorated and she was a meticulous house keeper. At her direction, I dusted every day, carefully lifting and shaking the starched doilies that she had under all her treasures. I brought flowers in from the garden and arranged them.

Every day but Sunday she did the washing in an old wringer machine, and I hung the clothes on the line. I was in charge of the garbage detail, carrying the trash out to a burn site and lighting it. Then I watched and poked the fire until it was consumed, all the while, enjoying the sun and sky. It was a perfect occupation for a thirteen year-old.

I didn't mind all the work because Auntie made it fun. She had a beautiful clear soprano voice, and as we worked she sang. *Amazing Grace* was a favorite of hers.

Aunt Thelma told me the first dirty joke told to me by an adult. She giggled for three days as she thought of it, and finally broke down and told me. The punch line is a tongue twister. Sixty years later, it is still my favorite dirty joke—maybe because it is the only one I remember.

Along with the songs and the stories, I sensed sadness. Aunt Thelma wished for something more. Perhaps it was to belong to the country club set that she'd had a taste of in the early years of her marriage. Or for Uncle Jack's status to be real rather than an illusive dream. Her desires crept out in conversation and the pains she took to cultivate the right people. I subscribed to my parents' philosophy that all people had value in their own right, not related to their social class. But I was careful not to express these views. I loved Auntie and, recognizing an undercurrent of sadness in her, I was careful of her feelings.

Uncle Jack was from Hornell and his sisters lived there. So I expanded my list of cousins to my cousins' cousins. One of them, Richard LaBarron, showed signs of being in love with me. I liked Richard, but I had no romantic feelings about him. He was just another cousin. But I did enjoy being admired.

The second year that I spent visiting my Aunt and Uncle, they had bought a small farm with fertile soil called muck. The soil was rich in organic matter. In fact, if it caught fire, it would burn. Since it was a drained lake bed, it was flat. The muck was surrounded by hills and the house, an older brick house, sat on the slope. There was water in the house but no bathroom. The outhouse sat further up the hill, against the woods.

Uncle Jack had dreams of growing vegetables to sell in all the markets in the surrounding area, and to some extent he succeeded in doing that. However as always, his dreams were more expansive than reality, and in spite of backbreaking work, they were never quite realized.

Living next to the muck land was like living near a pile of coal dust. When the wind blew, it carried the precious soil into all the cracks and crannies of the house. The summers I spent on the muck, my daily dusting was needed and Auntie's dirty clothes pile grew daily.

My cousins were very attractive young men. Billy's hair was so blond it was almost white and his eyes were deep blue. The hard work on the muck, crawling on his hands and knees to thin out the carrots, and hoeing the peas had muscled and bronzed his body. He was a bright young man and a skilled musician, playing the oboe.

In today's terms, my cousin was a *doll*. But because he was my cousin and I knew him so well, he was safe. I could practice being with a boy, dancing, and going to movies, without fear that I would say or do the wrong thing. He couldn't reject me; I was his cousin. And since I was his cousin, there was no sexual tension or concerns such as *should I let him kiss me*.

I did cause some trouble for Billy once. We went to a movie together. The person who took the tickets was the girl Billy was dating. As he handed her our tickets, he said, "This is my cousin, Flossie."

She looked me over and said, "Cousin? Yeah!"

So I inadvertently ended Billy's romance.

The second summer Jackie worked away from the farm and took some classes, so I didn't see as much of him as I did of Billy. He was a quiet, polite young man, handsome, but not the sort to send teenaged girls into a frenzy. He decided to join the Navy and and enter the submarine service. He needed to go to Buffalo to enlist. I traveled with him on the train for this important occasion. Then we saw the sights of the city. For a fourteen year old girl, this was a real thrill.

Every evening the boys and Uncle Jack went into the basement and washed and prepared the vegetables they grew for market. They not only worked hard during the day but in the evening also. Then Uncle Jack would sit alone in the kitchen until long after everyone was in bed, drinking beer.

One night at bedtime, Aunt Thelma and I went up to the outhouse. People were inclined to make visits such as this in pairs, hence two-holers. We heard something outside the little building, making noises and rubbing against the door. We concluded that it was my cousins, trying to scare us. When we returned to the house and berated them for trying to frighten us, they denied our accusations. Next morning we found bear tracks all around the outhouse.

There was one activity that stimulated the male bonding instinct among my cousins and their cousin, Richard. That was fishing. They fished in the stream that ran through the muck land. I begged to go with them. They assented and I got up at five in the morning for my first experience as a fisherman. They refused to let me use a pole and relegated me to the task of cleaning the fish. I never went again.

I was the only girl cousin on my mother's side of the family. But I did have female second cousins, the granddaughters of my grandmother's sisters.

Great Aunt Annie had been a nanny before she married. English born nannies were in demand among the wealthy of New Castle. One of her charges married Spencer Tracy. Aunt Annie felt that American children had poor manners and she set about trying to correct this fault in her grandnieces. Besides that, she was childless, and enjoyed our company.

Every summer, my second cousins, Betty and Barbara, and I were invited to spend a week at Aunt Annie's home. She cooked and baked for us and served up lessons in good manners along with the food. And we got to know each other well.

Uncle Taylor was a crusty old know-it-all. Years earlier when one of Annie's sisters asked why she didn't leave the miserable man, Annie had replied, "And do what? Work in someone's kitchen. Here at least I have my own."

We three great-nieces subtly baited Uncle Taylor. Then at night we'd giggle about what an ass he was. Gosh, I don't think that was such good manners.

One time we had raspberries for dinner. When I went to take a bite, I looked down at my spoon and saw a tiny green worm crawling out of a berry. "Ugh," I said, "a worm!" (Note: bad manners.)

"There is no worm," declared my great-uncle, "I cleaned them. Give them to me, I'll eat them."

So I handed over my berries and watched with great satisfaction while Uncle Taylor consumed the worm.

My father's brother James had survived the depression and he and his wife were reunited. The marriage eventually failed, but the family was together for a while and my parents visited occasionally. My younger cousin Marilyn came to stay for a time.

When Uncle Jim came, he always played the piano, wonderful old ragtime music. My father mentioned this to my violin teacher who taught music at the school in a near-by town and played for the square dances and Polish weddings. He asked to be invited next time Jim visited. Soon, every time Uncle Jim was at our house, we had a combo in the living room. The music teacher's brother played the sax and he and several others joined the group.

My school friend, Virginia Lee, invited me to join the Rainbow Girls, an organization related to the

Masons. I went through the initiation, which consisted of walking around a large room, stopping at various stations and being lectured to by older teens, dressed in evening clothes. I thought the whole thing was silly, but I wanted to join because of the formal dances that they held a few times a year.

When a dance was announced, I looked around at school and wondered who I could invite. None of the boys had dated me. Indeed, I hadn't had a real date, and I was reluctant to ask someone. Then I thought of my cousin's cousin, Jackie Pepe, who went to another school. He was my age, a good dancer and if he turned me down, I wouldn't have to face him every day at school. Jackie was my mother's brother's wife's nephew, just so you get the genealogy correct.

Jackie said, "Yes," to my invitation. I wore a white dotted Swiss dress, sort of a cross between Scarlet O'Hara and Snow White. Jackie's Father dropped him at our place and he brought a wrist corsage with him. As we headed out to my father's car, to be chauffeured to the dance, the Penwell boys were waiting in the driveway. Dale's eyes were warm and admiring. Young Johnny Penwell, who was ten said, "Geeze, Flossie, you're beautiful!"

We danced. I wasn't as smooth as Jackie who had four older sisters to teach him, but I passed. That summer, Jackie rode his bike from Hillsville, a few times a week to visit me. We talked and kissed. It wasn't a great love affair and with the exception of the kissing, it wasn't much different than my relationships with my cousins. When I went off to spend time at

Aunt Thelma's, Jackie wrote to me. Aunt Thelma saw the letter and didn't seem to approve. I didn't answer and that was the end of that relationship.

At school, I hung around with Virginia Lee. She had had one best girl friend, Vera, until I came along. Now Vera and I were rivals for Virginia's time. Ginny seemed to thrive on creating rivals for her affections. One time she had a party. I was away, so the account of what happened is second hand.

Ginny invited five girls, who just happened to be dating boys who were enamored of the hostess. So the girls invited these young men. The boys were unable to contain their hostility toward each other and there were a number of scenes. You can imagine what it was like for the girls who invited them. Ginny had a great time.

I knew what Ginny was like and I was willing to put up with it because of the positives. I enjoyed her company, and she was witty and intelligent. She was a great Glen Miller fan and had plenty of records and a record player. At home, we listened to classical music on the radio and and to Uncle Jim's ragtime. I loved listening to Ginny playing the piano. We stayed at each other's houses overnight. She had friends in New Castle who did interesting things, and she took me along to meet them. Most of all, there were always boys surrounding Ginny, and I enjoyed that. I had hope that one of them would notice the quiet brown-haired girl and turn away from the beautiful blonde who had initially attracted him.

My mother's younger brother, also a James, lived in Mt. Jackson, not far from the school. He was a barber. School had been difficult for him, so dreams of sending him to college were abandoned. He married a high school classmate, Eleanor, soon after high school and had one son.

Jimmy's shop was the community center of the little town. Men came to get haircuts, exchange gossip and do what my father called b___ s__t.

One of my freshman classmates was a tall quiet girl, named Esther. She was a little awkward and I don't remember that she had any special friends at school. Suddenly she began to tell us that she was dating fellows from the town who were out of school. Then she began talking about Jim Bear, her new steady boyfriend.

Jim Bear was Jim Baird, my uncle, and he was charged with statutory rape. The barber shop was closed and Uncle Jim went to jail. Years later when he was the executor of my grandmother's will, he cheated my Aunt Thelma out of her inheritance. When my mother was an old woman and close to death, she told me not to include his name in her obituary. I didn't.

The moral of the story: Not all cousins and brothers are worthy. But when they are, family ties bring a great deal of happiness.

Mother had returned to work. She was teaching fifth, sixth, seventh and eighth grades at Edinburg. She was much happier working than she had been when she was at home. She still didn't drive so Daddy had to take her to work and pick her up every day.

Daddy had gotten a job in a defense plant. It didn't last long. He thought his boss was a dope and he didn't hide his contempt. He developed a hernia and after he had surgery he didn't return to that job.

About a month after surgery there was consternation in our house. Mother thought she was pregnant. She was forty five. It seemed that after being separated for a week when he was in the hospital, Dad was so eager he couldn't wait until she inserted the contraceptive cream. Fortunately, her period finally arrived and the family settled back to normal.

By now, I was more relaxed about the fact that parents did it and Mother was open and easy to talk with.

One time she came home from visiting my grandparents. She kept giggling. When I asked what was funny, she told me that my grandmother who would have been in her early seventies was complaining that my grandfather who was close to eighty got amorous during the day. She was afraid that the neighbors would come to call and find them in a compromising situation. I remember thinking that if sex was as nice as my books say it is, isn't it nice that it can be indulged even when one is old. I hoped that the ability ran in families.

My own period finally arrived, a month before my fifteenth birthday. Now I was one of the crowd. When I told my friend Evelyn the news, she said, "Now, I'm the only one in the class who hasn't."

I soon learned to regret my eagerness to be a woman. I had severe cramps, so painful that I would sometimes faint. One time, I passed out while sitting on the toilet. Mother called Johnny and he helped her arrange my clothing and get me back to the bedroom. As soon as I recovered, I was faced with the embarrassment of having my brother see me that way.

My nipples became very prominent, because that is all there was, two large turgid nipples poking out from my sweater. Finally I did get some breast tissue to go with them.

It was difficult having a mother with such good taste. Her ideas did not correspond to the current fads, and anyway I wanted to choose my own clothes. I remember her saying to me, "Flossie, you have a long waist and a long body. But your legs are short. That makes you look dumpy. But if we move the waist of your clothes up a bit, that will give you a longer line and you'll look fine."

This was good advice and I've followed it ever since. But what I really heard was that I had a funny body and I looked dumpy.

Come to think of it, I've been resisting some of Mother's edicts about good taste ever since, even today.

Our last physical confrontation occurred during an argument about shoes. I had some new huaraches, Mexican sandals, and I put them on to wear to an evening church service.

Mother said, "You can't wear those to church. They are sport shoes."

I insisted that I would and she insisted that I wouldn't.

We were arguing in the hallway and she gave me a little shove toward my room. I fell to the floor and wailed. I could have caught myself, but I decided to go with the drama.

I wore the huaraches to church. They squeaked with each step. I was embarrassed. It was hard to have a mother who was always right.

I continued to do well in school as I moved into ninth grade. I managed to be first in most classes without much effort. I did have to work harder in the math subjects, but English and social studies classes weren't challenging. I had already read the books we studied in Literature and I read the paper and Life magazine. Since I had frequent sore throats, I missed a lot of school. If I were reading a good book, such as *Les Miserables*, I just stayed home.

If I ran into a problem in Latin, I could consult my father. He could translate the Latin on sight and had memorized some of the orations. I'm not sure when he learned Latin, since his formal schooling ended in third grade. He had been a devout Catholic when he was a young boy. Perhaps he learned it through the Church.

In class I was mouthy and opinionated, a real hand waver. My behavior was very different outside of class where I was quiet and shy. I tried to contain myself in the classroom, but I would be so stimulated by the subject matter and my classmates that I couldn't be quiet. Most of the teachers didn't seem to mind. But Miss Matthews did. She taught Latin and Literature. She refused to call on me and showered a lot of attention on the boys. Part of me resented what she did but I recognized that I did need to allow the rest of the class to have a voice.

One time Miss Matthews really made me angry. We were assigned to write a story. I wrote one based on what my father had told me about growing up in the anthracite region. I had seen the fall-ins, those pits that occurred on the surface when an underground passageway collapsed. When we had visited Uncle Pete we saw one that had swallowed a house. Stories about cave-ins and descriptions about what coal dust does to lungs were part of the family folklore. I worked very hard on my story about a little boy named Joe, and was proud to turn it in.

When the day arrived that the stories were to be returned, Miss Matthews called on three people to read the best stories. Mine wasn't one. I was disappointed and when I heard the other stories, I knew mine was better. After class I went up to ask her why I had been given a B when they received As.

She said, "Because you copied most of your story out of *How Green Was My Valley.*"

I had read the book and I told her that but this story was about the Pennsylvania coal fields where my father was raised and had worked.

She said, "I don't care what you say. You must have copied it." Then she picked up her papers and bustled off to Latin class, the stays of her girdle showing beneath her satin dress, and her heel clicking loudly on the cement floor. I was too amazed to protest further.

Half of me was flattered that she thought my story was so good that a famous author had written it. But I was also angry about being accused of plagiarism.

I considered telling my parents, but remembering the vehemence that accompanied Dad's vendettas, decided against it. However, I have wondered since, how different my career choice might have been if someone had encouraged me to write.

Mr. Spears was my favorite teacher. He taught the Sciences during the day and at night he worked as a metallurgist in the steel mills in Youngstown. He had a large family to support. His son Warren was my classmate and when we graduated he was the salutatorian. Our grades were very close. I've often thought how easy it would have been for Mr. Spears to inflate Warren's grades a little and deflate mine. He didn't, of course. In class he was extremely knowledgeable, very clear and fair.

At times in class I surprised myself—and my teachers. The teacher would raise a topic or ask a question, and into my mind and out of my mouth would come the answer. Now I would have no idea where this answer came from or how I knew. The question might involve a Greek myth, a Latin scholar, a German Philosopher or someone involved in a current event. It seemed as though my brain was like a vacuum cleaner, sucking up every bit of information that happened by and storing it. It can still happen when I am very relaxed. But over the years since my high school days, I've learned to keep my mouth shut. I'm afraid to blurt out the answer, because I might be wrong and then would be embarrassed. Isn't it strange that the brain that had absorbed so much, so easily, now can't produce the location of the car keys or a fellow board member's name?

Grandpa Tom was a great help when I studied Biology. The teacher gave us a list of trees and assigned us the task of making a notebook with the leaves of those trees and information about them. I asked Grandpa to help me. We walked back into the woods on his retirement farm. It was a small place, about ten acres where he kept one cow, six pigs, a large garden, a berry patch and fruit trees.

It was Autumn and the trees were in full color. He pointed out all the trees on my list and many more. He told me of their characteristics and uses. I was really impressed with his knowledge.

Then he showed me two small hills not far from the creek that ran through his property. He said that they were Indian mounds, left by an ancient tribe that once had occupied that region. He then went on to talk about the more recent tribes, the ones who had lived there and taken part in the French and Indian Wars. Grandpa was better than a history text book, and he was much more interesting.

Back at the house he showed me his collection of arrow heads and other artifacts. I had always loved Grandpa Tom and enjoyed his wit and gentle teasing, but now I respected his knowledge and his keen interest in nature and the things he saw around him.

It is interesting that my last marriage, the good one, is to a horticulturist who tells me the botanical names of all the plants we see, even the plants in the background of the movies. He also is interested in anthropology and other scientific subjects and picks up Indian artifacts from our farm. Both Grandpa and my husband have made the world a more interesting place for me.

About once a week the school had an assembly. Announcements would be made and lectures about proper conduct would be presented. Professor McCullough would be in charge. He was a tall man, well over six feet, with prominent brow ridges, reminiscent of a Neanderthal man. His voice was gruff and he was plain spoken. I don't know why he was Professor when all the other male teachers were Mister. I doubt that he had much more education than a master's degree, if that.

He would lean up against the stage and talk, and we students adopted a listening pose. He frequently talked about the dangers of venereal disease. Now I knew all about the subject—well, as much as my parents' books presented—and I knew that they really weren't toilet-seat diseases. But Prof, as he was called, went on and on about the awful things that could happen to you if you sat on a toilet-seat that had been occupied by an infected person. He never mentioned the activity that caused transmission most frequently, sexual intercourse. Of course we knew that is what he really was talking about.

He also rambled on about the war in Europe. He wasn't a veteran but he talked a lot about the horrors of war and the necessity of our staying out of it. I read the paper every evening and through my discussions— correction, arguments— with Daddy, I was certain that war could not be avoided. My opinion was far different than my classmates and I was learning to be careful of what I said in class. Most of the teachers and community were isolationists. Prof would lead us, with an off-key baritone in singing a song that expressed those feelings. It went something like:

I don't want to fight with the infantry,
Shoot the artillery,
Fly over Germany,
I want to be friendly.

I have often wondered what Prof thought when a few years later there were no male students older than seventeen in the school.

Pennsylvania was very cold in the winter. Since I had to walk to meet the school bus, keeping warm was a problem. Then too, the school was frequently cold and drafty. We were permitted to wear snow pants to school, but those bulky garments were removed with our coats and hung in the closets. There were no tights in the late thirties and early forties and wearing stockings meant wearing a girdle or a garter belt to hold them up. Besides that, silk stockings were expensive and rayon ones were baggy. Nylon had just been developed but it all went to the military.

There was no explicit dress code, but it was understood that girls wore skirts or dresses. I rode to school with two girls who also had chilled bare knees. We decided that we would wear slacks to school and see what happened. On the agreed upon day, I wore dark green wool trousers. I lasted about two classes. Then Professor McCullough came to the class and told me he had called my father to come and get me. He hadn't told him why. He scolded me for being unladylike. He said, "I might have expected it of the other two, but I thought better of you."

My parents were busy with their own lives, and I was reluctant to draw Daddy into my rebellion. So I spent the rest of the winter with chapped icy knees.

Prof's remark also told something about the social hierarchy at the school. The old families who attended Westfield Church were the chosen people. I was from an old family, but my father was an outsider and we lived at the edge of the township and went to church a mile down the road in Hillsville. The teacher's families, and school board members were also part of the upper end of society. Slightly below them were the attractive students who didn't fit in the top level. Virginia was one of these and I suppose I fit in there also because of my grades. Finally there were the students whose last names betrayed their Italian or Polish heritage and the families like the Penwells. These divisions were largely adhered to in dating. The casts for the school plays were selected from the top group, and it was clear that some teachers favored them.

I had grown up in Koppel with people from all the countries of Europe. I had enjoyed my Italian, French and Polish friends and classmates. My father told stories about his father immigrating to this country and seeing signs that said, "Dogs and Irishmen,

Keep off the Grass." The idea that all people are equal was drilled into me.

Hillsville was a mile down the road and more than half the population of that little town was Italian-American. Their forebears had been imported from Italy to work in the quarries. A few miles further away was Bessemer, inhabited by the descendants of Italians, Eastern Europeans, and Swedes. People from Hillsville spoke with an accent similar to the Brooklyn accent, and Bessemerites had an accent like Lawrence Welk. I liked the differences and resented the subtle hierarchy of the school. Perhaps that is one reason I made sure that I made the highest grades in the class.

One of the girls who had rebelled with me had an Italian name. The other was Marian Phillips. Her family lived in a house on the edge of a quarry. John was a friend of Marian's brother, Tom. I had visited their home with John and found them to be a friendly warm family. The Phillips were particularly attractive. They were part American Indian and had smooth olive skin. Their hair was black, thick and glossy and they all had beautiful light green eyes. I was determined to be friends with anyone I wished. Prof's remark made me even more determined.

I am glad to write that the hierarchy has vanished. The high school consolidated and all three communities have become one. The current principal and the faculty have names that originated in all the nations of the world.

I played violin in the orchestra. I was the last of the second violins and maintained the position. I had outgrown my 3/4 sized violin and the music teacher loaned me a full sized fiddle. The music I heard in my head, the sounds that made my heart soar, never matched the off-key squeaks that came out of my instrument. Besides that, the second violin parts never contained the melody and were boring. I had to drop chemistry in my Junior year because I had my tonsils removed and missed a month of school. The next year I took both Chemistry and Physics and had laboratory scheduled during the orchestra period. I returned the fiddle and ended my musical career. It was much more satisfying to listen to the NBC Symphony on the radio.

Since the school was small, everyone was in the choir. I listened to the opera every Saturday morning during the season, and loved it. But my own voice was thin and usually off key. I sang only when my fellow singers' voices soared to the rafters, and no one could hear me. Most of the time I moved my mouth and didn't sing. My friend, Virginia Lee, had a lovely voice. I enjoyed standing near her so I could listen.

I heard my classmates and others speak of someone and say, "She is smart but...". I was aware that I fit into that category. I was shy and inept in sports and music, but I was good in the classes that counted on my report card. I felt very grateful that I had inherited the talent to do that. Having seen my brother struggle in school made me aware that I was fortunate.

Chapter 13

Pearl Harbor, Falling in Love

Virginia Lee invited me to spend the weekend of my fifteenth birthday at her house. That birthday was December 6, 1941.

Most of Saturday was spent listening to Glen Millers arrangements on Ginny's scratchy record player or to the Chopin compositions that Ginny practiced on the piano. We gossiped about boys and school. It was a very pleasant day.

Sunday morning began as a lazy day. We had breakfast and talked about going to a movie. It was late morning and Ginny was in the bathroom. I was alone in her room listening to the radio.

Suddenly the music stopped and the excited voice of an announcer came on. "The Japanese have attacked Pearl Harbor!"

We were at war. The war had been in Europe, far away. We knew we would be into it eventually, but the country wasn't ready. Now suddenly the war had come to us. I wondered how it would change our lives.

Johnny came home from the CCC camp and went back to school. He was a grade behind me, in Eleanor Hoffmaster's class. I'm not sure his grades were any better but he seemed to get more out of school. He spent weekends and evenings working on an old motorcycle he was restoring.

My parents often dropped us off at the Legion Hall in Mt Jackson for the Saturday night square dance. The Legion Hall was a weather beaten wooden building, the entire first floor of which was a dance floor. The floor was splintered in places and gave a little when the music demanded that the dancers stomp. Joe Martin, my music teacher, his father and brother and a neighbor woman supplied the music and did the calling. The adults obligingly pushed us novices in the right direction and after a few dances we were reasonably proficient square dancers.

They also played slow dances, songs such as 'I'll Walk Alone' and 'I'll Be Seeing You'. I'd dance with Johnny a time or two and then the fathers of my classmates or my violin teacher would dance with me. The women would be showing Johnny new steps. The usual generational divisions didn't seem to exist— we all had fun together.

About the time the last song played Dad would show up and drive us home. I don't know why he and Mother never came to the dances.

Johnny finished his motorcycle and spent time in Bessemer with Donald Hardesty, nicknamed Ping, and Harold Heard. Harold was into motorcycles, too, and Ping was his sidekick. Ping had a sister, Marjorie, and Johnny liked her.

Margie was a year younger than I. She was a tall, blue eyed girl with brown hair. She walked with a slight limp, a residual of polio which she had as a young child.

Johnny began to date Marjorie and for some reason, my Mother sent me along with them. Margie and I had become friends but what guy wants a little sister along on a date?

I remember clinging to Margie, who clung to Johnny as we raced down a long hill on Johnny's Harley. There were no helmets and our hair streamed in the wind. Johnny turned his face as much as he could and Margie learned forward. Their lips locked together in a passionate kiss. I hoped that Johnny had his eyes open. I hung on and prayed.

One night Johnny dropped Margie off at her house and we rode home. Flew would be a more accurate description. I hung on and begged John to slow down. He responded by roaring the motor and going faster. I promised God that if he let me get off that machine alive, I'd never get on another motorcycle. John had chanced upon the perfect method to get rid of an unwanted chaperone.

I had seen Margie's brother, Donald or Ping, the year before. I had been in Bessemer, doing an errand for my Mother. I was walking up a hill past one of the lakes that had formed in abandoned limestone quarries. It was a beautiful summer day. There were no autos that afternoon and I walked slowly savoring the moment. A tall blonde boy, man, came striding down the hill, walking as if he owned the world.

The sun shone on his blonde hair and touched his tanned cheeks. When he got close to me he smiled and his dark blue eyes warmed. We each said "hello" and then he passed on.

Who was that? I wondered and when I got to my destination, I described the man. "Oh, that's Don Hardesty. Isn't he a handsome boy?"

I saw him again when I visited Margie's. He was in and out of the house and didn't pay much attention to me. He played basket ball for Bessemer and I went with Margie to the games. He also played the trombone in the school band and in a little dance band.

Male high school seniors were given a test by the Navy. They were looking for candidates for the V-12 program which was begun to produce naval officers. Qualified men would be sent to universities to study and when they graduated they would be commissioned as naval officers. Ping's grades had been unremarkable but he was one of two in Bessemer who passed the test. He would be going to college.

Ping's mother was a widow. Her husband had died eight or so years before after being chronically ill for some time with kidney disease. She had been left with six children, five sons and Margie. When I met the family the three older sons were working and married but at the time of her husband's death, only the eldest had finished high school and Lester was a baby. Mrs. Hardesty had taught school at one time. I'm not sure if she was qualified to teach when I met the family, but she was not working. One can only imagine what the depression years must have been for this family.

Johnny registered for the draft in February 1943 on his eighteenth birthday. A short time later, he was sent to Mississippi for training. He didn't write much, but Daddy wrote to him every day and I wrote often.

Dad had always been interested in current events. But when Johnny became a soldier, he became intensely preoccupied with everything regarding the war. Mother was concerned, of course, but she was busy teaching. We all became avid newspaper readers.

Dad's work continued to be erratic. At one point he applied for and was hired as a radio announcer. At the last moment he decided against taking the job. He did have a beautiful speaking voice. I have never heard poetry read as well as he read it. Several theater professionals had told him he should be an actor. When I was in class at school, if my father stopped by to see Professor McCullough I would know it. Although I couldn't hear what was said, I would catch echoes and reverberations and know that Dad was in the building. I've often wondered why he didn't take the job. Perhaps it was fear of failing, and that would have been a public failure.

When I was a junior and studying Chemistry, Dad asked me to bring my Chemistry book home. I did and he studied it for a week or so. Then he applied for a job as a field chemist for a chemical company. Actually he would be a salesman, but he needed to know enough chemistry to know what to recommend to the companies that would be his customers. He passed the test they gave all applicants, most of whom had degrees in Chemistry, and got the job. He kept it during the war years.

I studied my Chemistry book for a year and made a B. That was before grade inflation and there were only a few Bs and no As. Yet my father had mastered it without help in a very short time. If I were inclined to feel cocky about my grades—and I was occasionally—the mood was quickly dissipated when I compared myself with my parents.

I dated fellows I met through Ginny's contacts. I made sure I didn't date any of Ginny's admirers. I liked the boys I dated but I wasn't particularly attracted to them. I viewed the experience as practice.

There was one fellow who was a very good friend. Len Galanski had dropped out of school and was driving truck. He was a hard working, diligent fellow, not much interested in intellectual things. Often he would come by in his truck just as I got off the school bus, and would drive me home. We never dated but I considered him a special friend.

One day when he picked me up, he had some news. He had enlisted in the Marines and would leave in a few days. After basic training he was sent to the South Pacific. I wrote to him often and he responded, telling me about the hell he lived through on one island after another. I gave his address to Margie and they began to correspond.

Elmer Rummel asked me for a date and I agreed. Elmer had finished school and was working. I don't know why he wasn't in the service. My dad frowned on my dating older fellows, but Elmer was so shy, Dad knew I could handle him. We had very little in common. However he invited me to a party at his family's home.

Elmer was Margie Hardesty's first cousin. His sister, Verna, was a classmate of mine. Their family were farmers. I didn't think I would enjoy the party but I agreed to go. What a surprise, the party was wonderful. The family had moved all the furniture and rugs from the first floor of the house, creating a dance floor. The William's Boys, a tall handsome duo supplied the music and called the square dances. And did we dance!

For the first time in my life, I was the belle of the ball, the most sought after partner. Occasionally one of the Williams would leave the calling, singing or fiddling to his brother and break into the square to swing me off my feet. Every woman should have the experience. But the Rummels only had the parties once a year, and Elmer and I had too little in common to justify seeing each other until the next party. He found a nice girl his age who thought he was wonderful and, in a little while, was married.

I was the only girl in the Physics class. I didn't expect to like it, but it was one of my favorite classes. I liked the logic of it. Chemistry had seemed somewhat mysterious. I learned how certain compounds acted because it said so in the book or I saw then behave that way in the lab. But in Physics, it seemed that I understood why things were happening. I made a high A, the best grade in the class. Even though I had never put my nose under the hood of a car and the boys had all done that, I could tell anyone exactly how an internal combustion engine worked. It was fun beating out the boys in the grade race. But of course, this meant that I was less likely to date my classmates.

The atmosphere at home was more pleasant than it had been earlier. Mother was happy teaching, Dad was doing well at his job and there was a little money coming in from the limestone lease. For the first time in my memory, my parents were financially comfortable.

I continued to read at least a book a week in addition to my school work. I enjoyed the solitude of my room, a luxury I savored. The eaves on the house were wide and Grandpa John had trained wisteria on them. In the summer the flowers hung like heavy purple drapes. Occasionally I would look out and see the graceful form of a snake, twisted around the vine. I made sure the screens on my windows were firm so I wouldn't have an unwelcome visit from that sensuous fellow, and enjoyed watching him.

As I looked out the back window, across the lawn to the field beyond, I would see all sort of birds. Daddy had hung a bird feeder in a plum tree and in the winter, I could see the red cardinals flash by and listen to their song.

Before long, my cousin Billy Lusk was an Air Force medic in the South Pacific. His brother Jackie was in the submarine service. Mickey Fisher and Jerry

Sainsot, Aunt Maymes son, were in the Army. Later Uncle Bill's son, Bill, would join them. I wrote to them all. I tried to make my letters interesting and entertaining. They wrote back begging for more, and I obliged.

As the boys at school became eighteen, they would disappear into the service. The male portion of the class became smaller and smaller. Bob McFate went into the Navy and there were no more joyous sleigh rides.

The wartime food rationing caused no problems for our family. My mother had proved that she could make a meal out of nothing during the depression and we could always eat Daddy's soup. We had our own vegetable garden and plenty of the fruit from our trees. Grandpa Tom had pork in the smoke house and he gave us some occasionally.

However, gasoline rationing was a problem. Dad had to take Mother to and from work and travel in his work. When I was sixteen, I wanted to learn to drive, but there was no gas to be wasted, so my lessons were postponed. I suspect, too, that Dad's position as the family transportation manager was one he wasn't eager to share.

Margie and I attended a Memorial Day parade in New Castle at the end of my Junior year. School bands from all the surrounding towns took part. Donald 'Ping' Hardesty marched in Bessemer's band, playing his trombone. He looked wonderful in his uniform. The parade ended near the County Courthouse and Margie and I managed to be waiting there. Ping seemed to notice me for the first time and I was thrilled.

Within days, we were seeing each other every day. Ping had just graduated and was scheduled to leave for Dartmouth College on July first. He'd ride his bike to my place, or I would ride mine to spend time at his. I was supposed to be visiting Margie as I had for more than a year, but I had a new goal in mine when I pedaled my bike to Bessemer. We swam in one of the quarries, took long walks and kissed and kissed some more. We exchanged profound opinions and worked hard to impress each other.

After a few weeks, we swore eternal love and he asked me to marry him when the war was over and he returned. I said yes.

Were we in love? How can one measure what one feels at sixteen? He was beautiful, handsomer than any of Ginny's admirers. He was smart and he would soon be a naval officer. He was sexually attractive and I loved to kiss and cuddle with him. It was especially nice since he never pushed to go beyond kissing and hugging.

Ping left and I became a Navy Sweetheart. We wrote long letters every day, full of expressions of love. I no longer was interested in other fellows, I was being true blue to my Sailor.

Ping was experiencing all the adjustments required of any first year college student. In addition he roomed with regular college men, from upper class families. I suspect that the son of a poor widow from a little Pennsylvania town had some problems fitting into that group.

In his letters, he described marathon bridge sessions that lasted a whole weekend. He found a bowling alley in town and spent a great deal of time there. In speech class, he had a difficult time coming up with subjects, until one day, in desperation, he described how cement is manufactured. Cement manufacture was Bessemer's main industry and Ping's father had been the Millwright at the plant. The teacher and the class were very interested and he received an A. The next week, his topic was the manufacture of bricks and after that he moved on to describe the strip mining of limestone. These were industries located in Bessemer, places where older brothers and neighbors had worked. It seemed that a working class boy did have something to offer the class at an ivy league school.

I began my senior year that fall. At Christmas, he sent me an expensive watch. My peers at school considered this a pre-engagement gift. I already considered myself taken. If any fellow was interested in me, I drove him away with my constant talk about my wonderful boy friend. Besides because the boys were drafted as soon as they were eighteen, there were fewer and fewer boys in our class.

In his letters, Ping wrote that he was more dissatisfied with life at Dartmouth. He talked of wanting to go to sea, and really make a contribution to the war, rather than staying in college. Between the lines, was the message that the classes weren't going well. Decisions about which students would go into the Navy as ordinary seamen, and who would stay in the V-12 Program and become officers were to be made at midterm.

At midterm, he wrote that he had made the decision to go to sea. I was sure that he had no choice, that he had failed some of his classes. His devotion to bridge and bowling had seemed to me to be more compelling than his desire for an education.

I was disappointed and ashamed of my feelings. I believed then, as I do now, that all people have value and that a person's worth is not measured in wealth or status. Was I not a terrible person to allow the fact that my Love would not be a naval officer to taint my feelings for him? I also firmly believed that each person should choose his own occupation. I struggled to suppress my disappointment.

Ping came home for a month's leave before he was to report to boot camp. We spent every evening together. Mostly we sat around in a borrowed car and necked. We still stayed above the neck, but the atmosphere was more highly charged with sexual feelings than it had been before.

I was struggling with another question. What was I going to do with my future? Of course, I planned to marry Ping, but first I wanted an education and an occupation that would enable me to support myself. My parents' experience during the depression had made the importance of this clear. Daddy was well read and had a first rate mind, but it was my school teacher mother who had supported the family. Besides all this, I was curious about the world and felt that I had only begun to learn what I needed to know.

So between the hugs and long passionate kisses, we discussed what I would do. I didn't want to be a teacher. My teachers were almost all old maids or men. Mother had reminded me that she was not an old maid and she was a teacher, but somehow the image didn't appeal to me. I was interested in journalism because I liked to write, but was afraid that it was too difficult a field to assure a decent living. I had no desire to be a starving writer.

We mentioned nursing and both vetoed that. I didn't think I could do the things nurses need to do. Ping had heard all the stories about nurses that were passed around in the services. Nurses were women and they were officers. The mixture of being unavailable to enlisted men and in a superior position produced feelings that led to unpleasant stories.

I had talked with Miss Mathews about what career I might chose. She said, "Flossie, I think you are a scholar. You love to learn for the sake of learning, not for any particular usefulness to you."

I was upset by her reply. What I heard was a variation of what the kids said when they said, "She is smart, but....."

I also thought of my father, the brightest man I knew, who could quote most of Shakespeare, the famous national documents and poetry, yet had trouble earning a living. Now I know how right Miss Mathews was. Learning was and is, one of life's great pleasures.

Ping went off to boot camp at Sampson Naval Base, and later to Fort Lauderdale, Florida to range finder school. Range Finders calculate the position of the big naval guns so that they will hit the selected target. My disappointment vanished, or was pushed down, and I again extolled the virtues of my sailor to anyone who would listen.

Chapter 14

I Choose a Career, Graduate and Leave Home, Johnny Lands on Omaha Beach

The Spring of my senior year I was constantly worried about what I would do the following year. If I were the Valedictorian, I would be given a scholarship to Geneva College. But even if I were first in the class, what would I study?

One day I walked into the girl's restroom. There on the wall was a poster showing a smiling young woman in a gray uniform, trimmed with red. She was wearing a beret with a silver emblem on the front. The lettering read, "Nursing is a Proud Profession, Join the Cadet Nurse Corps." I took one of the fliers attached to the poster.

Free nursing education was being offered to qualified women who joined the Cadet Nurse Corps. In return they were obligated to engage in essential nursing, in military or civilian settings, for the duration of the emergency. Interested people selected the nursing school they were interested in and applied. If they were accepted, they could join the Corps.

My inner dialogue went something like this. "All the men are in the service, why not me? Nursing is a useful occupation and nurses always seem to have work. It would be good preparation for raising a family. Why spend my parents' money for college when I plan to work only until my children are born?"

The reservations about nursing that I had expressed to Ping didn't seem important, when compared with all the positives. I decided to become a nurse.

Mother was amazed at my attitude about work and motherhood. I was much more conservative than she. Although few people would know that, she was such a soft spoken woman. The war had fostered conservative attitudes about the women's roles, at the same time that women were running the factories and doing the work of the absent men. This was viewed as temporary, a necessity until the boys came home. Then women would settle down to raise families and bake apple pies. Now I am also amazed that in spite of my nontraditional family, I eagerly accepted the prevailing attitude.

We had no counselors at our school and my teachers knew very little about the health professions. So I asked the only people who I thought might know, doctors. Mother's doctor recommended the Hospital of the University of Pennsylvania in Philadelphia. Another mentioned the Presbyterian Hospital in Pittsburgh. No one mentioned schools that offered college degrees and I had no idea that they existed. I never considered the two schools at the hospitals in New Castle. I wanted to leave home and see a life outside of Lawrence County, Pennsylvania.

I applied to both of the suggested schools. They required that I take a pre-nursing exam that was being given to Cadet Nurse Corps applicants at a hospital in New Castle. It was an all day test. I happened to be a good test taker and enjoyed the challenge. The young women who took the test with me were, for the most part, very upset by it. I kept my mouth shut and didn't express my feelings—I had finally learned something I should have learned several years before in high school.

I passed, with an excellent score, and was accepted by both schools, although the one in Pittsburgh wouldn't take me until I was eighteen. HUP accepted me for the September class, dependent on a satisfactory interview.

Mother and I took the train to Philadelphia for the interview, the first train ride that I remember. Mother was worried most of the way. She had started her period and was afraid the things she had packed for this emergency wouldn't be enough to contain her heavy flow. Mom's worries always irritated me. I reassured her. Somehow in my irritated state, I never noticed how smoothly she handled the details of the 400 mile trip, the taxi at the station, the hotel, and finally getting us to the hospital for the interview.

When I met Miss Lynch, the head of the school, that lovely lady suggested that my Mother leave me there, take the bus downtown and enjoy the day. I began to object, thinking that Mother couldn't manage alone. Miss Lynch misunderstood my hesitancy and assured that I would be all right without Mother.

As I look back, I am amazed at the way I underestimated my capable mother, the woman who supported the family all through the depression, and knew so much about diverse subjects such as geology, astronomy and sociology. Years later when my own teenaged daughters treated me as though I were slightly retarded, the memory of how I had regarded my own mother offered me a little comfort.

The Hospital of the University of Pennsylvania School of Nursing accepted me. My future was assured. I had chosen my life work and my life partner. Each decision was made with very little information and no experience.

The senior prom was approaching and there were no men to escort many of us. Those who turned eighteen year had left shortly after their birthdays. Ping was in Florida and I was being true. Ginny had finally chosen a love from among her many suitors, but Bud Hilke was in an Army camp in the South. Ginny, three other girls, and I decided to attend together.

I wore a plaid taffeta dress with a white bodice and my mother's most precious jewelry, a white sapphire bracelet. It was one of the few luxuries that remained from the prosperous days when my parents first married. The prom was held at the Castleton Hotel in New Castle. Ginny's step father drove us there and another father picked us up. I danced with the male teachers, even Mr. Stunkard who worked his decided limp into a dance step. Ginny spent the evening in the phone booth, tearfully trying to call Bud at his army camp. I lost mother's bracelet and neglected to tell her until it was too late to advertise for it. We did our best, but the evening was a bust.

Mr. McCullough, Prof, the school principal, came into our home room one morning near the middle of May, walked to the blackboard, and proceeded to write our grade averages on the board. We were graded by the percentage method, and at that time, 80% was a good average grade. It was considered a C when a C was perfectly acceptable. My score was in the low nineties, the highest in the class, and Warren Spears was just a few tenths of a percent below me. I was the Valedictorian and Warren was the Salutatorian.

I labored over the speech I would give at graduation. I knew that high sounding phrases were expected, but they seemed so foreign to my usual speech, I couldn't imagine myself uttering them. Mother suggested that Dad help me. I heard him tell mother that my speech was pretty dull. I refused his suggestions. Finally I came up with the theme about the opportunities created by the war. I do remember one phrase, "Steam rolling necessities of war...." And I did slip in a few florid bits.

The auditorium was packed that evening in late May when the class of 1944 graduated. I stood behind the podium to deliver the speech. I had stopped being embarrassed with the high sounding phrases I had inserted into the memorized text, and spoke with conviction and sincerity— I hoped. About half way through I looked down into the audience and by chance found my parents. Uncle Jim Fisher and his wife, Hilda, were with Mother and Dad. Their four faces were turned up toward the stage and glowed pride and pleasure.

I was so moved that I paused. As I began again, I heard, Miss Matthews, my prompter, hissing the line I had skipped. But not to worry, no one listens to the exact words of graduation speeches. The small auditorium shook with applause when I finished.

I've forgotten the speech and many other things, but more than fifty years later, my memory holds a perfect picture of the radiant faces of my family.

There were twenty-seven diplomas stacked on the table beside Professor McCullough and the school board president. But far fewer graduates marched across the stage to receive them and endure Prof's crushing handshake. Our classmates had been drafted as soon as they were eighteen and were in training camps in this country, the South Pacific or in England, preparing for the invasion of Europe.

Johnny was in the 163rd Combat Engineers. With his mechanical talents it was a perfect assignment for him. While they were training in this country he invented a bolt that hooked the pontoon bridges together more efficiently. At the time of my graduation he was in Overton, England waiting for the invasion. He had trained with the Rangers and the British Commandos.

On June 6,1944 the 163rd landed on the Omaha Beach at low tide. Their job was to clear the land mines so that the rest of the Army could land on the beach without having to contend with them. Most were visible. Fifty years later when I questioned him about it he said, "The Germans weren't so smart. They expected us at high tide".

After the landing, he fought in the Battles of Normandy and Brittany. He was at St. Lo and Bastogne. He told me, "We passed Paris real fast".

His outfit was a specialized one that was moved around where needed. It was attached to the 1st, 3rd and 9th Armies. John seldom wrote, so it was difficult to guess where he was in Europe and what he was doing.

When the news of the invasion came over the radio, it seemed as if the whole country held its breath. I'm not sure I appreciated the reality of it and I tried not to think of what Johnny might be facing. Daddy was immersed in all the details of the War, and in the European sector particularly. He pored over all the newspapers and Life magazine. There was a picture of a soldier running across a swinging bridge at St. Lo. Although his face was obscured by his helmet, Dad was sure it was Johnny. "Look at his hand, that nervous hand John has."

Mother didn't obsess about the details; she just worried.

Ping had finished training in Florida and was sent to San Francisco. We hoped he would be able to come home before he went to sea, but that was not possible. Each day we sent long ardent letters to each other. He played a lot of cards and bowled as he waited. Finally he boarded a troop transport and was sent to the Pacific Islands where he was assigned to a landing craft tender.

My last summer at home was one of preparation. Mother helped me put a wardrobe together, now that I was a young woman, rather than a school girl. At times, her innate good taste in clothes was irritating, but even while I protested, I appreciated her input.

That summer, I walked around the house, yard and garden and said goodbye. I sensed, correctly, that I would never live there again. This house had been home. The other houses and the apartment had just been places to put our furniture and stay a while. Even though I had moved to the brick house only five years before, I had lived there briefly as a three year old, and visited it virtually every week until we moved there. I knew every tree , and the taste of all the fruit. and which bush produced the most fragrant roses. Both Dad and I were sure that the birds that nested in the trees were yearly tenants.

I gave my stuffed animals, even my precious bunny, to some neighbor children and packed up my Shirley Temple doll to save for the daughter I would have someday. At night, I opened my window screen enough to admit Timmy, my black tomcat, and invited him to spend a few stolen nights in my bed.

Ginny was going to Westminster Choir College in Princeton, New Jersey, where she would study organ and voice. We promised to see each other since we wouldn't be so far apart. I did visit a few times when I was in Philadelphia. Then she transferred to a college nearer home and married Bud when he was discharged.

Eleanor Hoffmaster was a year younger than I. She was already making plans to attend the University of Michigan the following year. Margie Hardesty had another year in high school and no particular plans for the future. My male cousins and friends had already gone to the service.

The summer of 1944 I spent saying goodbye to my childhood.

As the day to leave drew closer, I packed my clothes in the footlocker the school had suggested we buy. In among the clothing, I put Ping's framed graduation picture. I wore his class ring on a chain around my neck. All of Ping's letters, tied in bundles with ribbons went into the chest. I asked Dad if I could take *One Hundred and One Famous Poems,* the book I used to learn to read. With Mother's permission, I slid in a small blue glass vase.

I was to report at nine in the morning at the apartment house that the hospital had just bought to house the largest class they had ever admitted. That meant I had to leave on the train for Philadelphia the day before, take a cab to the hotel where I would stay the night. In the morning I would get a cab to take me and the foot locker to the new dorm. I was glad my mother had gone with me for the interview. She had shown me how to accomplish that.

Mother had to be at her school, the morning I left, so I kissed her and said goodbye in the kitchen. Daddy drove me to the station in Mahoningtown. It was a small station, outside the town. We stood in the morning sun on the deserted platform with the foot locker beside us. The breeze stirred dad's thinning gray hair, but he still was a handsome man, even to my critical seventeen year old eyes.

Dad kept clearing his throat. This was something he did when he was moved and close to tears. I heard the same sound when his favorite law school teacher, Judge Gestner, died. I noticed it when we attended sad movies or listened to very bad news on the radio. There weren't any tears, but I knew my Daddy was crying. And I was glad that he found it painful to see me leave.

The train arrived and the conductor helped Dad move the footlocker up the steps. I turned to give Dad a hug and he kissed me, his mustache tickling my cheek. The train was full of servicemen but I found a seat with an elderly woman. As we pulled out from the station, I looked out the window, waved to Dad, and said goodbye to my childhood.

I was sad, but I was excited about the future and grateful that in leaving home I took so many good things with me.

ORDER FORM

Name_____

Address_____

City/State/Zip_____

Phone_____

Enclosed is my check for $15.45 ($12.95 for **ROCK GARDEN FLOWER** and $2.50 for shipping.

**Silver Tree Books
Box 707
Silverton, OR 97381**

e-mail: florencehardesty@aol.com

☐ Check here if you would like the book signed by the author